WHAT REALLY GOES ON IN SOPHOCLES' THEBAN PLAYS

Charles B. Daniels
Sam Scully

089682

University Press of America, Inc.
Lanham • New York • London

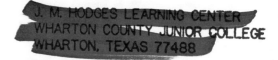

Library of Congress Cataloging-in-Publication Data

Daniels, Charles B.
What really goes on in Sophocles' Theban plays / Charles B. Daniels,
Sam Scully.
p.   cm.
Includes bibliographical references and index.
1. Sophocles. Oedipus Rex. 2. Seven against Thebes (Greek
mythology) in literature. 3. Greek drama (Tragedy)--History and
criticism. 4. Antigone (Greek mythology) in literature. 5. Oedipus
(Greek mythology) in literature. 6. Sophocles. Oedipus at Colonus.
7. Sophocles. Antigone. I. Scully, Sam. II. Title.
PA4413.07D36   1996   882'.01--dc20   96-6787 CIP

ISBN 0-7618-0304-1 (cloth: alk. ppr.)

Contents

I

Oedipus Rex

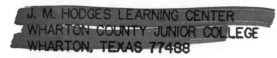

II

Oedipus at Colonus

Part 1

III

Antigone

IV

Oedipus at Colonus

Acknowledgements

Thanks go to Aris Argyriou for his enthusiastic and critical encouragement, to Keith Glading for his patient instruction in computer manipulation, and to Sandra Chellew for just too many things to list. We gratefully acknowledge a grant from the University of Victoria that made publication possible.

Preface

The Greek Theater and Sophocles

On first encounter, whether in reading or performance, Greek tragedy seems to many to be highly verbal and static, formalistic and even markedly alien. This is an explicable and valid reaction, in that it emphasizes differences between the Greek Theater and our own, between Greek culture and our own. It is a salutary reaction that should help us to guard against the naive equation between the ancient Greek world and our own, an equation too readily made by the nineteenth and early-twentieth centuries.

Yet difference is rarely absolute, more often a matter of degree. Thus while much of Greek culture and of the Greek theatrical world is foreign to us, Greek tragedy also deals with universal human experiences in ways that can communicate immediately to us, its modern audience.[1] It is able to engage us because ultimately it is in its own terms deeply theatrical and dramatic, and at once intellectual and emotional.

The purpose of this preface is to provide some contextualization for the argument that follows: in particular, to offer some pointers to the

---

1. These first two paragraphs owe a great deal to the discussion by Taplin [1978], pp. 7-8.

distinguishing features of the classical Greek theater and a succinct account of what is known about Sophocles and his theatrical career. These remarks are dogmatic and often reductionistic. Correction and elaboration can be found by consulting the works referenced in the notes.[2]

The first distinguishing feature we might observe is the very place of tragic drama in the communal life of fifth-century Athens. Formal dramatic productions were associated with festivals dedicated to the god Dionysus, and tragedies were included in the City Dionysia, a festival of great prominence in the political and cultural life of the state held annually in middle to late March.[3] Thus tragic drama was part of the worship of divinity, a sacred event. But it must be stressed that tragedy was not itself a ritual. It often makes use of the rituals of actual religious practice — for example, of prayer, hymn, and supplication — but it lacks the repetitive character and the repeated elements that mark ritual.[4]

Nor does the context of religious festival entail that we should view dramatic performances primarily as religious worship. That context also has its social and political dimensions. John Gould rightly points out the analogy with the great religious contests of the Greek world, such as the Olympic games. In both settings, the Athenian theater and the stadium at Olympia,

---

2. On the Festivals, see the revised Pickard-Cambridge [1968]; on the Theater, see Gould [1985].

3. For a brief summary of the "festival context", see Rehm [1992], pp. 12-19. Note that the "context" has left no mark on the plays themselves.

4. See Vickers [1973], pp. 41.-2, and Taplin [1978], pp. 161-2.

the endemic and potentially disruptive competitiveness of ancient Greek society was validated and sanctified by dedicating conspicuous display of competitive achievement to the worship of the gods.[5]

The Athenian dramatic performances, like the athletic games, were contests played out before the community. Dramatists, actors, and the wealthy citizens who at great personal expense sponsored the productions were all competing for victories that would be recognized in public record and in private monument.

This competitive dimension of the Athenian theater is but one of numerous features that set apart the Athenian theatrical productions from what we are familiar with in the modern theater. Another is the city's deep involvement in the organization of the festival and of the dramatic performances, all assigned as a major responsibility to the *archon eponymous*, the chief magistrate of Athens (an assignment that, given the generally secular nature of the archon's responsibilities, should again make us wary of stressing the religious context of performance at the expense of the secular and the political).[6] Imagine the Prime Minister of Canada or the President of the United States playing a similar role!

Each summer, shortly after assuming his one-year appointment, the archon nominated the financial producers (they were called *choregoi*) who, as part of the Athenian institution of "liturgies", performed this function as a public service. Most of their expenses were to do with the payment and training of the chorus (probably twelve in the plays of Aeschylus; fifteen in the later plays of Sophocles and Euripides). Little is known about the selection of plays, except that the archon listened to readings from their works by the applicant dramatists. The archon then assigned to the three successful poets their financial producers, and production commenced.

---

5. Gould [1985], p. 265.

6. Rehm [1992], pp. 20-30, provides a good summary of the "production process".

The playwright was almost always his own director and producer. The Greek phrase closest to the English "directing a play" was *didaskein choron*, "to teach a chorus". This usage underscores the central importance, in the production, of choral training which was intensive and spread over months. In the actual performance the chorus occupied a prominent place. The physical center of the performance space in the classical Greek theater is the huge circular area of the dancing floor (the *orchestra*) — at Athens at least twenty meters in diameter — where the chorus moved, singing and dancing the odes which divide the acts (the *epeisodia*) of tragedy.[7]

No feature of Greek tragedy is more intractable than the chorus. It is frequently difficult to discern the relations between their songs and the action that commands our attention. The choruses in Sophocles' Theban plays will receive little discussion in this book because their songs are, more often than not, pitched on a different plane, differentiated from the specific concerns and incidents of the action. Or so it seems to the modern reader and spectator. Yet perhaps that differentiation is a product of our ignorance of the facts of original performance, of their music and choreography, and of our inability to appreciate choral singing and dancing, for the Greeks, "such an integral part of many communal occasions, religious and secular-festivals, weddings, funerals, victory celebrations, for example".[8]

The rehearsals for tragic productions must have been time-consuming, as song, dance, and a complex text were learned. The same group played the chorus in all four plays presented by a dramatist. At some point in the process the dramatist must also have begun work with the three male actors who (from as early as 458) shared the speaking parts in the four plays. The fifth-century theater saw an increasing importance in the prominence of actors — initially the tragedian himself acted the most important roles — and with the institution of the prize for best tragic actor in 450 or so came another

---

7. On the *orchestra*, see Gould [1985], pp. 266-68.

8. Taplin [1978], p. 13; this paragraph paraphrases his discussion.

typically Athenian institution, the use of the drawing of lots by the three competing tragedians to pick one of the three actors chosen to compete that year. The expenses of that actor, together with his assistant actors, were in all likelihood assumed by the state.

It is convenient here to touch upon the most basic convention of the ancient theater, the masking of actors and chorus. The causes and effects of this masking are not easily summarized. Masking is clearly linked to the massive size and open nature of the ancient theater. It serves to project the role of a person and, indeed, his *persona* to the audience, and, together with costume, to establish instantly some essential markers such as gender, age, and status. The masks also allowed a single actor to play multiple, divergent roles in the same play. But such practical benefits do not begin to exhaust the meanings of so durable a convention. It has been noted that the Greeks used the same word, *prosopon*, for "face", "mask", and "dramatic character", a word that literally means something like "towards the eye", and that Sophocles exploits these meanings in *Oedipus Rex*, where Oedipus "returns with a new mask that shows his gouged eye-sockets, an image of his true character, a man who was blind to his own identity."[9]

Masking, of course, removes much that we view as central to acting, indeed, the whole repertoire of facial expressions; but all this was unavailable to the Athenian actor in the huge fifth-century theater which must have shaped the whole style of acting. Thus actions, gestures, and movements must have been such as to be visible to a spectator at least fifty meters from the actors, and there is evidence to support the intuition that the clarity and the strength of the actors' voices must have been all-important (the comparison with their modern operatic counterparts performing in large, albeit enclosed opera-houses seems irresistible). Thus there are testimonia that Sophocles stopped performing in his own plays because of his weak voice.

This emphasis on voice is directly linked to the central prominence in the Greek tragedies of the spoken word. Fifth-century Athens witnessed the birth of rhetoric, itself both a cause and an effect of the

---

9. Rehm [1992], p. 40; also Gould [1985], p. 276. In general, on masking, see Taplin [1978], pp. 14-15 and Gould [1985], pp. 276-78.

political culture and of its preoccupation with public discourse which in their turn leave their marks on the tragedies. If the language of tragedy is in a grand style, often removed from ordinary speech, and if its delivery was commensurately grand, it is, above all, certain that vocal control and clarity were the primary prerequisites of the actor in the large, open-air theater.[10]

The lengthy process that commenced each summer and the months of preparation culminated in the productions each March at the City Dionysia. Those single performances produced victors: the names of the winning dramatist-director, actor, and *choregos* were inscribed on the official lists. To provide judges for the contest, the names of male citizens in attendance from each of the ten tribes were put into a jar, and one was drawn from each jar just before the performances began. At their conclusion, the judges voted anonymously. Once again, we should note, Greek tragedy was located in a festival and competitive setting that was a fixed point in the city's calendar.

The religious festival and its dramatic performances were acts of the community, and that communal dimension is confirmed by the size of the audiences, anywhere between 12,000 and 15,000, that attended the performances on each of the three days. From some time early in the fifth century, the tragedies at the City Dionysia were presented in an area dedicated to Dionysus on the south slope of the Acropolis. The spectators sat on the hillside in this natural theater, though there may have been some limited seating of wood or stone at the front.[11] The dominant aspect of the theater is one of open, public space, in clear contrast to the closed theaters with their proscenium stage to which we are so accustomed. The open ancient theater demands of its audience

---

10. On "voice" in the ancient theater, see Gould [1985], pp. 280-81.

11. The current remains in the theater of Dionysus in Athens date from the early Christian era, including the stone seats and semi-circular *orchestra*. Reconstruction of the fifth-century theater is made extraordinarily difficult by the many changes made to the theater over succeeding centuries.

a different kind of imaginative engagement that is prompted and controlled by the words and actions of the performers.

This communal dimension should not be taken to imply some simple relation between the tragedies themselves and the contemporary political world. Rather, the plays repeatedly engage, through the traditional tales[12] they represent in new guises, the political as well as religious and social concerns and the tension of that contemporary world. The Athenian tragedians are not the plodding moralists or theologians that earlier criticism so often portrayed. On the contrary, they explore moral and religious questions without sitting in judgment or offering facile answers. The thought of Aeschylus or Sophocles is everywhere in his plays; rarely, if ever, is it reducible to simple propositions.

So too with their approach to the political ideologies and issues of their day.[13] Greek tragedy repeatedly returns to the conflicts betwen the claims of state and household (see, for example, Sophocles *Antigone*), to the complexities of political action and decision-making and to the ambiguities of civic life and discourse. If from time to time a figure such as the Athenian King Theseus, in, for example, *Oedipus at Colonus*, exemplifies right political actions, such conduct is not a matter for Athenian complacency — the citizenry would have expelled Oedipus — and our attention is quickly switched to the conflicts and threats created by the actions of Creon and Polyneices. If the world of the tragedies seems foreign, all too often the human experiences they represent are immediately familiar and accessible and thus can engage us in direct and uncomfortable ways.

If our evidence about Athenian theater and about the society which cultivated it is always less than we could wish, the same is even truer

---

12. These tales were not fixed, but took different forms and versions. The different versions of Oedipus' career are illustrative: on this, and on the general issue, see Taplin [1978], pp. 162-64.

13. See now Goldhill [1990] for the argument that the tragedies constitute a questioning of the terms of the contemporary civic discourse and ideology.

when we contemplate our ignorance about the dramatists. What do we know about Sophocles?[14]

He was probably born in the first decade of the fifth century, about 496, and died in about 406, in the last years of the Peloponnesian War. An ancient source claims he wrote 123 plays; titles of some 118 are known; and a mere seven have survived. He first competed at a tragic festival in 468, when he won first prize and beat Aeschylus. The number of victories over his long career is variously reported at 18, 20, and 24, and it is also reported that he never placed lower than second.

Most of the surviving plays cannot be firmly dated. For only one, the *Philoctetes*, do we have a secure date (409). It is unlikely that any of the other extant plays is earlier than the 450s. The modern consensus, based on largely stylistic grounds, puts *Ajax* earliest and before the *Antigone*, which was perhaps produced in 442, if we can trust the evidence of the ancient first hypothesis to the play that its success won Sophocles the generalship in the campaign to the island of Samos. Many would place *Trachiniae* next, on no strong evidence, and then *Oedipus Rex* (after 429, but in the 420s, if the plague at Athens is reflected directly in the play). The *Electra* is usually thought to belong to the decade before the *Philoctetes*, while there is ancient evidence that the *Oedipus at Colonus* was produced posthumously in 401 by the dramatist's grandson, also called Sophocles.

All this uncertainty makes it impossible to contemplate any useful account of Sophocles' development.[15] We must also be very wary of

---

14. Our knowledge depends on the ancient *Life of Sophocles*, which is preserved in a number of medieval manuscripts, and on a mixture of bits of material, composed mainly of anecdotes or other brief mentions by ancient scholars. On Sophocles, see Buxton [1984], pp. 3-7 and Easterling [1985], pp. 295-99.

15. The ancient sources contain much about his contributions to the formal development of tragedy: for example, introducing the third actor, increasing the chorus from twelve to fifteen, beginning the practice of presenting plays on different stories rather than connected trilogies and so on. See Easterling [1985], p. 297.

making too much out of the ancient anecdotes about him, many of which very probably draw on stock patterns and events or are based on inferences from his plays to his supposed experience. One source, for example, reports an argument between the old poet and his son, Iophon, an argument which was settled when Sophocles read from the *Oedipus at Colonus* and so refuted the claim that he was senile. This story looks too much like the quarrel between the old Oedipus and his son Polyneices to be convincing.[16]

The ancient biographical tradition is particular insistent on Sophocles' piety and his public service, and there has been a tendency in modern scholarship to make a great deal of these alleged features, and particularly his piety, in efforts to make sense of Sophocles' presentation of the relationships between men and gods. But this naive imposition of alleged biographical fact immediately founders when we confront the deep complexities that define the dramatist's portrayals of those relationships.

In fact, notwithstanding the vast scholarship of the modern era, there is no critical consensus about Sophocles; indeed, in his case that scholarship is distinguished by the diversity of often conflicting approaches and analyses. The interpretations that are set forth in this book are a further contribution to this continuing debate.

---

16. See Buxton [1984], pp. 4-5, on this anecdote and for the evidence about piety; for persuasive scepticism about such anecdotes, see Lefkowitz [1981].

Introduction

Two of Sophocles' three Theban plays, *Oedipus Rex* and *Antigone*, are, if not the best known, among the best known dramatic works ever written. Why, then, should yet one more interpretation of them be added to twenty-five centuries' accumulation of criticism? We have two reasons for doing so: First, the literature has not resolved problems about these plays, simple problems that continue to puzzle readers. Second, much that has been written about them, especially about *Oedipus Rex*, is not just wrong, it is 180 degrees wrong. Tradition has it, for example, that Oedipus is a highly intelligent man. As we read *Oedipus Rex*, the story demonstrates the exact opposite: Oedipus is anything but a highly intelligent man.

As its title indicates, our principal aim in this book is to make clear what really happens in these plays. To accomplish this, we explain and make use of the Aristotelian categories of plot, character, and thought — although only one of the three plays, *Oedipus Rex*, qualifies unequivocally as an ideal Aristotelian tragedy. We approach the plays as arm-chair detectives. Facts and possibilities are gleaned from the text. We then try to come up with motivations, and interesting and plausible explanations.

In working on a project like this, it soon becomes clear that very different pictures of what is going on emerge when a play is viewed in isolation, than when it is set in the context provided by companion works written by its author. Thus we have made it our practice, when studying each play, first to pretend that the others have not survived. This produces what we call the *narrow interpretation* of the events in the play. Then we try to see what must be altered when the play is viewed against the background of what takes place in the other two works. This we call the *Theban context* of the play.

That it is even legitimate to read the events of one play as carrying on a story started in another is a matter of controversy — although we would hate to have to inform authors who wished to write interlocking plays that the laws of literary interpretation forbid it. Yet in order not to scatter our arrows too widely by pursuing this debate here, we set the matter aside by asking readers to proceed hypothetically by assuming that the events of *Oedipus at Colonus* do follow upon those of *Oedipus Rex* and those of *Antigone* upon those of *Oedipus at Colonus*. We also treat each play in isolation, so if the assumption of a continuity of events between plays is somehow wrong, the forgiving reader will still find something of value in these pages.

The discussion of each play begins with a Chronology of Events. The importance the Chronologies have in determining what exactly does happen in each play — the main goal of this book — cannot be overemphasized. The events listed in them are drawn, with one exception, from speeches in the text. The exception lies in *Oedipus Rex*. The particular riddle the Sphinx posed to Oedipus when he arrived in Thebes is not detailed in the text. We accept the riddle tradition attributes to the Sphinx: What is two-legged, three-legged, and four-legged?

This book is divided into four parts. The subject of Part I is *Oedipus Rex*. Why is Oedipus — to all appearances the premier solver of mysteries in Thebes — the last major character in *Oedipus Rex* to see the truth? Contrary to what much of the literature would have readers believe, we show by examining Oedipus' history that he really has no great problem-solving talent at all. He is an arrogant man, filled with false pride in the cleverness and intelligence he mistakenly thinks he possesses. He seeks out and basks in the limelight and prizes public recognition and adulation. He has a trigger temper and is extremely defensive — to the point of disloyalty to those closest to him. We argue that Oedipus is not an innocent victim. He definitely has himself to blame for the terrible events that overtake him at the end of the play.

Part II explores the relationship between *Oedipus at Colonus* and *Oedipus Rex*. The events revealed in *Oedipus at Colonus* call for additions and even amendments to the chronology of *Oedipus Rex*. *Oedipus at Colonus* provides us with a satisfying resolution to several issues that remain unresolved at the end of *Oedipus Rex*. We are not only present when Oedipus dies, we also learn what has happened to

him in the interim. Time and suffering have had their effects. Oedipus
is a changed man. He is much less subject to explosive fits of rage and
at all to violent ones. He no longer seeks center-stage, but has come to
value privacy and discretion.

As regards the responsibility he bears for the events chronicled in
Oedipus Rex, *Oedipus at Colonus* is two plays. On the narrow
interpretation, it portrays Oedipus as an innocent and long-suffering
martyr. In the broader, Theban context, however, we see that Oedipus
has reached a limited, though still imperfect rapport with himself. As
sometimes happens as the years pass, time has gilded his memory and
given him a comfortable, although flawed, view of himself and the
events in his life.

Part III is devoted to *Antigone*. The immediate problem *Antigone*
poses is a strange one: why is it that Polyneices' body actually gets
buried three times during the course of the play? After all, the play is
presumably about the burial of a body that is *not* buried. Also, we once
again have a work which on the narrow interpretation is one play and
in the broader Theban context another.

If *Oedipus Rex* and *Oedipus at Colonus* had not survived, it could
easily be argued that *Antigone* is a model Aristotelian tragedy, having
not one but two protagonists, Creon and Antigone herself. On the
narrow interpretation, both qualify as Aristotelian tragic heroes; both are
portrayed as good people who display great fallibilities. Creon, like
Oedipus himself, is extremely defensive and will not listen to what he
does not wish to hear. Like Oedipus, he is pig-headed and arrogant.
Like Oedipus, he fails to distinguish himself by intelligence or
cleverness. He speaks too much. He blunders badly. On her part,
Antigone seems as much interested in self-righteous oration and
posturing as she is in burying her brother, a deed which, the events of
the play make clear, she could accomplish clandestinely without
difficulty if only she would back down and just be quiet.

Against the background provided by *Oedipus at Colonus*, however,
a good case can be made that *Antigone* does not qualify as an ideal
Aristotelian tragedy at all, because it has no paradigmatic tragic hero.
Creon is disqualified immediately because in *Oedipus at Colonus* he is
shown to be evil. And the behavior that seems to indicate a fallibility
in Antigone's character can, in the wider Theban context, be read as the
best course of action possible in a singleminded effort on her part to

right wrongs and to defend herself and her sister by frustrating Creon's machinations and bringing him down.

Finally, just as *Oedipus at Colonus* works to satisfy our curiosity about how Oedipus fares after the terrible conclusion of *Oedipus Rex*, *Oedipus at Colonus* illuminates *Antigone* by giving us a detailed lesson in getting right what Creon in *Antigone* turns upside-down — respect for the gods, custom, and tradition.

Part IV looks at *Oedipus at Colonus* on its own. *Oedipus Rex* is an ideal Aristotelian tragedy in both the narrow interpretation and the wider Theban context. *Antigone* is an Aristotelian tragedy on the narrow interpretation and what might be called a *sacrificial* or *heroic* tragedy against the Theban background. *Oedipus at Colonus*, while serious, is not a tragedy in either sense. What kind of play is it? It is a play about acting correctly. Oedipus has one important choice left in his life: who is to receive the foretold mysterious benefits which are to come to those who give him shelter and bury him? Oedipus does his best to act correctly in dying, despite attempts to thwart his will, and to see to it that the people who really deserve the blessings he has to bestow do receive them.

Of the co-authors of this book, Charles Daniels is responsible for the interpretations given the plays. Sam Scully has produced the Preface and the accurate and unpretentious translations[17] upon which the interpretations are based.

---

17. The Greek text is normally that printed in the new Oxford Classical Text edited by Hugh Lloyd-Jones and Nigel Wilson (Oxford: 1990).

Tragedy According to Aristotle

One can hardly find a general discussion of classical Greek theater that does not pay homage to Aristotle's *Poetics*. This book is no exception. The *Poetics* is of special importance here, because in it Aristotle refers to Sophocles' *Oedipus Rex* several times and cites the play approvingly as a paradigm of dramatic tragedy.

According to the *Poetics*, dramatic tragedy has six components: plot, character, thought, diction, melody, and spectacle. The plot is the action dramatized — that is, those events which are enacted on stage and are common to all performances of the play. Thus the plot of a play must be distinguished from the events that the audience learns about from the dialogue as the play progresses. The personages in the play express in their dialogue what they know and believe. They discuss events that have taken place at other times and places and are not themselves enacted on stage. These events Aristotle includes in the component *thought,* because they come to be known as the play unfolds by what the play's characters disclose of their thoughts in dialogue.

Let us call the incidents of the plot, plus all those events we do not witness but know about from what characters of the play say, the *story* of the play. In limiting *plot* in this way to the actions dramatized on stage and putting the remainder of the story in the category of *thought*, we believe we are being faithful to Aristotle's text. If this is a mistake, we beg the reader to bear with us and give us the distinction we draw between *plot* and *story* anyway, since for present purposes one key question we shall be addressing and attempting to answer is: what actions are really dramatized in the *plot* of *Oedipus Rex*? Thus, in the Chronology of Events that follows, the story of *Oedipus Rex* includes almost everything in items 1 through 27, while the plot includes 11 through 27 but excludes 1 through 10.

Aristotle leaves no doubt that he considers plot to be the most important component of dramatic tragedy. As he says, plot contains the changes of fortune, discoveries, and reversals, and it bears the play's identity through the variations and differences there inevitably are in different performances of it.

Aristotle believes that in tragedy a good plot must show the hero's fortunes to decline from good to bad. This change in fortune must spring from the actions of the hero himself, but not from any villainy on his part.

> 13. Following upon what has been said above we should next state what ought to be aimed at and what avoided in the construction of a plot, and the means by which the object of tragedy may be achieved. Since then the structure of the best tragedy should be not simple but complex and one that represents pitiable and fearful incidents — for that is peculiar to this form of art — it is obvious to begin with that one should not show good men passing from good fortune to bad. Such situations are not just pitiable and fearful; they are incapable of fitting resolution. Nor again wicked people passing from bad fortune to good. Such a situation is the most untragic of all, being neither fitting, pitiable, or fearful. Nor again the passing of a thoroughly bad man from good fortune to bad fortune. Such a turn of events might be fitting, but it is neither pitiable nor fearful, the one being a case of a man who does not deserve his misfortune and the other of the man who is like ourselves — pity for the undeserved misfortune, fear for the man like ourselves — so that the result is neither pitiable nor fearful.[18]

It is clear in context that by "good men" we can read "men who are pre-eminently virtuous and just". The problem with a situation in which

---

18. Daniels, *et al*, [1992], p. 213. The interpretation of this passage reflects the view argued for in [1992] that the reference of the terms "pity", "fear", and "catharsis" in the *Poetics* is only incidentally to actual emotions of readers or viewers of tragedies and is meant primarily to demarcate kinds of dramatic events, incidents, and actions *in* tragedies, *fearful* and *pitiable* ones and ones that lead to *fitting resolutions*. The literal translation of this passage used in [1992] appears in the Appendix.

a pre-eminently virtuous and just man passes from good fortune to bad is that, because he is *pre-eminently* virtuous and just, it is not through a fault of his own that he comes to grief. There is no appropriate or fitting resolution to such a calamitous turn of events, since if justice really were to prevail it would not happen to a pre-eminently virtuous and just man in the first place.

Aristotle directly sets forth the ideal for tragedy:

> The fine plot must then be single and not, as some say, double; and the change must be not to good fortune from bad but, on the contrary, from good to bad fortune, and it must not be due to villainy but to some great fallibility on the part of such a man as we have described, or of one who is better rather than worse.[19]

The protagonist must be good, not a villain, but not pre-eminently good.

In the case of plays like *Oedipus Rex*, in which the story goes well beyond the confines of the plot, it is an interesting and valuable exercise to ask oneself what exactly does happen in the plot. What does take place in the plot of *Oedipus Rex*?

The audience attending to the plot of *Oedipus Rex* has a particularly difficult problem to solve: Why is Oedipus, the most famous and to all appearances the best solver of mysteries in Thebes, the last major character in the play to solve the mystery of his own life? The aim of this book is to throw some light on this and other questions about the play: is Oedipus simply a victim of his fate, or, given the kind of person he is shown to be as the play progresses, is it reasonable to think that the part he plays in bringing about his own downfall is more than merely passive, and that the smarter of the gods — Apollo, for instance — might well have predicted, rather than pre-ordained it?

Oedipus does not kill his father and marry his mother on stage. These actions are not part of the plot; they are part of the given — which Aristotle warns, as a highly unlikely concurrence of a highly unlikely pair of events, does not belong among the actions of a good

---

19. Daniels, *et al*, [1992], p. 212.

play, but outside it (outside the plot, that is, but inside the story). The plot of a good play must be seen to march along to the drumbeat of necessity and inevitability and must not contain improbabilities.

Now, given Oedipus' circumstances when the play begins, what tragic flaw, what "great fallibility" does he display, what error does he commit *on stage*, from the time the action begins to the time it ends? All the evidence we cite in attempting to answer this question, and questions like it, will come from the text, with a single exception: the riddle the Sphinx posed to Oedipus and Oedipus solved. The dialogue of the play does not say what the Sphinx's riddle was, but tradition takes it to be: What is two-legged, three-legged, and four-legged?

For Aristotle, the ideal tragic hero is one who is neither pre-eminently virtuous and just, nor downright evil, one who is better (or better off) than most, and yet who, through some great fallibility, causes his own downfall. Oedipus is not evil; he is clearly no Iago. We show that Oedipus is definitely not pre-eminently virtuous either and that he does display great fallibilities during the course of what we see on stage, surprising ones given his reputation, both within the play and in the critical literature. Pitiable and fearful circumstances await Oedipus as the play opens. Given the kind of person Oedipus is, his relentless march to the horrific final scene is assured. Yet another sort of leader in such circumstances might escape the worst of Oedipus' humiliation and suffering, while still arranging that Thebes be saved from the plague.

Our discussion of *Oedipus Rex* is organized under three headings: Investigative Talent, Public Posturing, and Character Flaws. These headings represent topics that are by no means exclusive. Oedipus, and in the last play of the Theban "trilogy", his brother-in-law, Creon, and his daughter, Antigone, go out of their way to take unnecessary public stances that work to their own detriment and undermine the very ends they wish to achieve. This tendency toward public posturing is definitely a flaw of character, but it plays such an important role in the plot of *Oedipus Rex* that it merits its own separate discussion.

To start off, however, we ignore Plot and focus instead upon Oedipus' vaunted cleverness and investigative talent. We show that the popular idea among scholars that Oedipus possesses a keen, penetrating mind is utterly wrong. That it is wrong comes out in unexpected and tantalizing bits as the play progresses, when we slowly learn what has taken place before the dramatized action of the play begins. Thus, to evaluate what is really going on on stage in *Oedipus Rex*, we must first take a hard look at the episodes of the story that precede the plot. Then, when we know better the kind of man Oedipus really is and what he has and has not done earlier in his life, we can see and appreciate much more clearly what is taking place on stage before our very eyes.

I

Oedipus Rex

Chronology of Events

1. An oracle tells Laius and Jocasta, King and Queen of Thebes, that their son will kill his father.

2. Laius has the ankles of his three-day-old son pierced and bound together, and Jocasta gives the infant to a servant to kill by exposure on Mt. Cithaeron. The servant gives it instead to a shepherd, who, in turn, gives it to Polybus and Merope, the childless King and Queen of Corinth. Polybus and Merope name the baby "Oedipus" and raise him as their son.

3. Troubled by persistent rumors that he is not really their son, Oedipus consults the oracle at Delphi, where he is told not who his parents are, but that he will kill his father, marry his mother, and father children by her.

4. In an attempt to keep the oracle's prediction from coming true, Oedipus resolves to leave Polybus' kingdom. During his wanderings he meets his real father, Laius, and Laius' retainers at an intersection where the road from Thebes forks to go to Daulia and Delphi. The retainers force Oedipus off the road

and, as Laius' carriage passes, Laius knocks him on the head with a stick. In angry retaliation Oedipus kills Laius and all his retainers save one who, unbeknownst to Oedipus, escapes — the very same servant who saved his life by giving him to the shepherd.

5.   Because Thebes is beset by the Sphinx — part woman, part dog, part bird, a monster that poses riddles and kills and eats those who prove unable to solve them — the death of Laius receives only cursory investigation. The sole survivor claims that the attack on Laius' party was the work of a band of men.

6.   Oedipus arrives in Thebes and saves the kingdom from the Sphinx by answering the riddle it poses: what is two-legged, three-legged, and four-legged? Answer: man, who first crawls, then walks, and finally uses a cane. When the Sphinx hears the answer, she dashes herself on the ground and dies.

7.   Oedipus, now a hero, is made king by the Thebans and marries Laius' widow, his own mother, Jocasta. The survivor of the massacre of Laius and his party begs Jocasta to send him back to the countryside to be a shepherd. She does.

8.   A long time passes[20], enough for Oedipus to have four children by Jocasta. Two of them, the boys, are teenagers when Oedipus Rex opens.

9.   A plague falls upon Thebes, and a blight spreads over its fields.

10.   Oedipus sends Creon, Jocasta's brother and his trusted friend, to the oracle at Delphi to find out what can be done to end the plague. At Creon's suggestion Oedipus also summons the blind prophet, Teiresias.

11.   As the play opens, the citizens of Thebes appeal to Oedipus to save them a second time.

---

20. *Oed.*   [Laius] gone from sight by a deadly stroke?

   Creon.   The measuring of years would take you far back into the past.

(OT 560-61)

12. Oedipus reveals that he has sent Creon to Delphi and makes a public promise to do whatever the oracle demands to stop the plague.

13. Creon returns from Delphi and explains the oracle's answer to Oedipus and the assembled citizens: to end the plague, the murderer of Laius, someone born and now living in Thebes, must be exposed and exiled or killed.

14. Oedipus undertakes to solve Laius' murder and punish his killers. He proclaims to his subjects that all who have knowledge of the slaying of Laius will be rewarded if they come forward and punished severely if they do not. The murderer, Oedipus announces, will be exiled, not killed if he comes forward and confesses.

15. Oedipus expresses surprise that Laius' killing was not investigated at the time it happened. The chorus reports a rumor that Laius was killed by travellers on the road. All but Oedipus and the chorus exit.

16. Having been summoned twice, Teiresias reluctantly appears and at first refuses to help Oedipus' investigation. This unwillingness to speak about it angers Oedipus, and he insults and goads Teiresias to come out with what he knows about Laius' death, which Teiresias finally does — saying that Oedipus' hot temper should be blamed. Oedipus, now steaming mad, accuses Teiresias of plotting the killing himself. Teiresias then bluntly charges Oedipus with being Laius' killer. Oedipus reacts by accusing the absent Creon of trying to overthrow him and paying Teiresias to blacken his reputation. Oedipus goes on to claim that Teiresias is a fake, unable to come forward with the answer to the riddle of the Sphinx at the time it was really needed. Teiresias replies that Oedipus is the one who is really blind. In a series of riddles ironically directed to Oedipus, the proud "solver" of riddles, Teiresias tells the truth about Oedipus and foretells what will happen. Teiresias exits.

17. News of Oedipus' charge of conspiracy has reached Creon, who arrives to defend himself. Oedipus accuses Creon to his face of having conspired to murder Laius and of paying Teiresias to blacken his name. Creon defends himself by pointing out that he has no motive to attempt to usurp the

throne and that Oedipus has produced no evidence to support his charge. By virtue of being the queen's brother, he already has power and respect, without any of the onerous and undesirable responsibilities which come with having to rule. Why, asks Creon, would he wish to change that? Oedipus stubbornly sticks to his charge and claims he must act swiftly to defend himself against Creon's conspiracy.

18.   Jocasta appears and tries to mediate. Creon swears he is innocent. Oedipus draws attention repeatedly to the choice: if Creon's and Teiresias' innocence is believed, then the public must conclude that he, Oedipus, is guilty. Under the urging of Jocasta and the chorus Oedipus sullenly relents. The chorus urges Jocasta to take Oedipus inside and speak to him in private, but this advice is ignored. Creon exits.

19.   Oedipus goes on to tell Jocasta that Teiresias, as Creon's pawn, has accused him of murdering Laius. Jocasta explains that Oedipus need not worry about Teiresias' words. She relates that an oracle once prophesied that Laius' life would be taken by his own son and that Laius had the infant killed by exposing it in the mountains with its ankles pierced and tied together. She concludes that since the infant died, the prophecy was wrong; Laius did not die at his son's hands. He was killed by unknown robbers at a fork where three roads meet. So much for oracles and seers, she concludes. The oracle Laius received proved wrong, and Teiresias' prediction should not be given credence either.

20.   Oedipus is now troubled by memories of his own deeds at a crossroads and asks Jocasta for more details about where Laius was killed and what he and his companions looked like. From Jocasta's response, Oedipus realizes that he may well have killed Laius. He then asks Jocasta about the lone survivor. Jocasta tells him that the survivor, upon returning after Oedipus had acceded to the throne, begged to be sent back to the countryside to be a shepherd. Oedipus speaks of the couple he regards as his own parents, the Corinthian king, Polybus, and his Dorian wife, Merope. He tells of the rumor he heard about his not being their real child, what the oracle at Delphi prophesied when he consulted it, and how thereafter he had

carefully kept away from his parents' home in Corinth. He then recounts his meeting with a man in a carriage at the junction of the three roads and how in angry retaliation he killed the man and his retainers.

21.   Oedipus now takes very seriously the possibility that he killed Laius. He bemoans his fate: to be exiled from Jocasta and his children for having killed Laius, his wife's former husband, and because of what the oracle told him, to be exiled as well from his home and parents in Corinth. He claims to prefer an anonymous death rather than to suffer the ignominy of having killed his father, Polybus, and married his mother, Merope. As a last resort, Oedipus seizes upon the one hope that remains, the one bit of possible evidence that can prove his innocence of Laius' murder — whether the retainer who survived the massacre will testify that more than one person did the killing. Oedipus sends for the man.

22.   A messenger arrives from Corinth and announces that King Polybus has died of old age and that the Corinthians wish to make his son, Oedipus, their king. Jocasta rejoices in a further disproof of oracles: Oedipus clearly did not kill his father, Polybus. Oedipus, however, still fears the remainder of the prophesy — that he will marry his mother, Merope — and explains to the messenger that he cannot return to Corinth and why. The messenger then tries to show Oedipus that his worries are groundless: A long time ago, recounts the messenger, when he worked as a shepherd, he was given the infant Oedipus by a Theban shepherd, and he in turn gave Oedipus to the childless Polybus and Merope. Merope is not really his mother! He has nothing to worry about! To back up his account the Corinthian mentions the scars and swelling on Oedipus' ankles and remarks that this was how he got his name — "Oedipus", it is suggested, means "swollen foot". Oedipus demands that the Theban shepherd be summoned to confirm the Corinthian's story. It transpires that the man has already been sent for; he is the lone survivor of the killing of Laius and his attendants.

23.   Jocasta has by now realized the truth and tries to dissuade Oedipus from continuing to pursue his inquiries. Oedipus ac-

cuses her of trying to stop his investigation lest it reveal that he is the son of a slave and that she has married beneath her station. Jocasta exits.

24.   Laius' old servant, the shepherd, arrives and is identified by the Corinthian messenger as the man from whose hands he received the infant Oedipus. The messenger reminds the shepherd of their acquaintance and of the infant. It is clear by this time that the shepherd knows the truth about Oedipus. Reluctantly and under duress, the shepherd confesses that he knows about the infant and that it came from the house of Laius. The queen gave it to him to put to death because of a prediction that it would grow up and kill its father. The shepherd simply did not have the heart to do away with the baby and felt it would be safe to give it to a foreign shepherd to raise somewhere far away from Thebes.

25.   Oedipus goes into the palace, finally acknowledging who he is and what he has done.

26.   A messenger reports to those outside that Jocasta has hanged herself and Oedipus has put out his eyes with brooches from her dress.

27.   Oedipus, blind and bleeding, comes on stage. Creon appears and lets it be known that he has arranged to consult the oracle again about what should be done with Oedipus. He then orders that Oedipus be taken inside so that he does not have to grieve and suffer under the public gaze. Oedipus begs that Jocasta be given a decent burial and that he be allowed to embrace his young daughters. His two sons, he says, are old enough to fend for themselves. Creon has already had the children brought out and agrees to look after the girls. *Oedipus Rex* ends.

Investigative Talent

As the play opens a priest speaks for the suffering citizens of Thebes who have come to petition Oedipus for his help:

> It is not because we judge you as ranked equal with the gods that I and these children sit on the steps of this altar, but because we judge you to be the first of men, both in the chances of life and in dealings with immortals. For it was you who came to the town of Cadmus and released it from the tribute which we were paying to the cruel singer . . .
>
> (OT 31-36)

> . . . we entreat you, all we suppliants, to find some help for us, whether you know it perhaps by having heard a message from some god or from a man; for I see that it is for the experienced that the bringing together of counsels is most effective. Come, best of mortals, raise up our city! Come, take care! For now this land calls you Saviour because of your former endeavour . . .
>
> (OT 41-48)

Oedipus, the priest tells us, is the first of men at getting to the bottom of mysteries. This is his reputation, gained in particular, indeed *entirely*, from his having solved the riddle of the terrible Sphinx years before. As the Chorus says

> For once in the sight of all the winged maiden came against him, and in that test he was seen to be wise and loyal to the state. Therefore he will never be found guilty of wrongdoing by my judgement.
>
> (OT 507-12)

17

Oedipus, it turns out, has already acted by sending his brother-in-law, Creon, to Delphi to ask the oracle what should be done. At Creon's suggestion, he has also summoned the blind prophet, Teiresias. Teiresias, too, has the reputation of being a solver of mysteries:

> But here is one who shall convict him [Laius' murderer]. For here they
> lead the godlike prophet, in whom alone of men the truth lives.
>   (OT 297-99)

When Teiresias arrives, he angers Oedipus by an unwillingness to help expose Laius' murderer. Then, when Teiresias is in turn angered enough by Oedipus' goading and insults to speak to the point, he accuses Oedipus himself of killing Laius and hints that he is unnaturally married — the exact same prophecy, we find out later, that Oedipus heard years earlier from the Delphic Oracle. Teiresias predicts further that Oedipus will end up being despised by all. Incensed, Oedipus responds by crowing about his victory over the Sphinx and ridiculing Teiresias for his failure to defeat her:

> For, come, tell me, on what grounds are you to be seen as a true
> prophet? Why, when the singer, the hound, was here, did you not say
> something that could deliver these people? Indeed, the riddle, at least,
> was not for anyone who came along to interpret clearly, but needed
> prophecy; this art you were not seen to have, either from birds or as
> known from any god. But I came, Oedipus who am supposed to know
> nothing, and I stopped her, hitting the mark by my mind and learning
> nothing from birds.
>   (OT 390-98)

A few moments later, we have the following interchange:

> *Oed.* How excessively riddling, how opaque are all your statements!
> *Teir.* Well, are you not the most skilled in finding their meaning?
> *Oed.* Reproach me with that in which you will find me great!
> *Teir.* It is this very fortune, however, that destroyed you.
> *Oed.* But if I saved this city, I do not care.
>   (OT 439-43)

Without doubt Oedipus has bought his own reputation for wisdom and is not above preening himself for his investigative genius. But is his reputation truly deserved? Does Oedipus really have a talent for solving mysteries he can rightly take pride in? As he departs, Teiresias presents an ironic challenge to Oedipus' supposed genius by delivering his final prophecies as a series of riddles — which leave Oedipus stumped.

Actually, up to his confrontation with the Sphinx and subsequently as well, Oedipus in no way distinguishes himself as a clever solver of mysteries. As the play unfolds we learn of six riddles concerning Oedipus' earlier life which Oedipus either chose to ignore or has failed completely to resolve.

The first puzzle Oedipus might have taken up comes to our attention only as the play arrives at its conclusion, just before the denouement:

Mess.	Your own ankles might give evidence.
Oed.	Ah, why do you speak of this old suffering?
Mess.	I freed you when your feet had been pierced.
Oed.	Yes, I took a terrible disgrace from my infancy.
Mess.	So from this fortune you were named who you are.
Oed.	For the gods' sake, was it my mother's deed, or my father's? Tell me!

(OT 1032-37)

The mystery Oedipus as a child and youth shows no signs of having probed is: what caused the scars on his ankles that gave him his name and distinguished him from his playmates? Who, indeed, would do such a thing to a child? We, in the audience, are offered no reason to think that the young Oedipus tried to discover the explanation.

We do know that when a drunk jeered at him saying that he was not his father's son, Oedipus became very angry, but kept his temper, went to Polybus and Merope the next day, and questioned them closely, receiving their repeated assurance that he was, indeed, their son:

For at a banquet a man, too full of strong drink, over the wine claimed that I was not my father's child. I was angry and I barely restrained myself for that day. The next day I went up to my mother and father and questioned them. They were angry because of this insult with the man who had let the word fly. So I was comforted on their part, . . .

(OT 779-85)

His adoptive parents clearly wished him to believe he was their real son, so it is reasonable to assume they made up a story to explain the scars on his ankles — a story that did not, of course, reveal the truth, that raised no suspicions in Jocasta's mind when she heard it, that satisfied him, *and one his highly touted investigative acumen did not penetrate.*

The second puzzle to touch Oedipus' life we learn about from his own mouth slightly over halfway through the play: were Polybus and Merope his real parents?

The drunken man's jeers rankled, and when the rumor spread that he was not their son, Oedipus went to the Delphic Oracle to learn the truth. His decision to consult the oracle to learn the truth about his origins in no way distinguishes him as a solver of mysteries. Oracles were ubiquitous and consulted by everyone, including Oedipus again when he sends Creon to ask for advice about the Theban plague. After consulting the oracle about who his parents were and having it raise the stakes on the answer without providing the question with an answer, Oedipus seems to have done nothing further in the way of trying to ascertain what the answer really was.

In the same passage Oedipus goes on to disclose a third mystery: how Oedipus behaved in light of the puzzling response the oracle did give and the answer it did not give, when he asked it if Polybus and Merope were his real parents.

> Unknown to my mother and father I went to Delphi, and Phoebus sent me away not honoured in the things for which I came, but for wretched me he clearly announced other horrors and sorrows, that I must sleep with my mother and I would show a family unbearable for mankind to look upon, and that I would be the killer of the father who sired me. When I had listened to this, from then on I measured the location of Corinth's land by the stars and went into exile to a place where I should never see the disgraces of my cruel oracles fulfilled.
>
> (OT 787-97)

Remember now, the reason why Oedipus consulted the Delphic Oracle in the first place was that there was some question in his mind as to whether Polybus and Merope were his real parents — enough doubt to cause him to go to Delphi to try to put it to rest. *Yet even though Oedipus says the oracle gave no answer to the question of his*

parentage, he went ahead and behaved as if it had confirmed that
Polybus and Merope were his real parents!

G.M. Kirkwood makes an interesting observation in another context
that sheds light here.

> The revelation of Oedipus' anger and his too ready suspicion of Teiresias
> have implications for the character of Oedipus that are not to be
> disregarded. Toward the end of the scene there is a subtle and most
> revealing display of Oedipus' egoism. A reference by Teiresias (436) to
> the parents of Oedipus catches the king's conscious ear, though the
> foregoing declarations of his guilt have found him apparently deaf.
> Oedipus is for the moment all attention (437), and we think that now he
> must learn his parentage. But the prophet answers enigmatically (438),
> and Oedipus reproaches him for doing so (439). Teiresias asks if solving
> enigmas is not Oedipus' special skill (440); and this reminder of his
> triumph over the Sphinx so engrosses the king's attention that he forgets
> all about his original question and the moment of possible revelation
> passes unfulfilled. ([1988], pp. 68-69)

What is of most interest for present purposes is implicit in Kirkwood's
observations: Oedipus is easily distracted. He does not have a pier-
cing, focused intellect. When he asked the oracle who his parents were,
the oracle did not answer the question, but rather went on to make
terrifying, puzzling predictions about horrible things that would happen
in the future. In this situation, hearing the mind-riveting prophecies the
oracle was making, Oedipus may at the moment simply not have
noticed that it failed to answer the question he posed and only realized
this later.

If one takes the oracle seriously, as Oedipus gives evidence of doing
by exiling himself from Corinth in an attempt to avoid the fate it set out
for him, one intelligent course for him to take in this attempt is not to
kill any older man or marry any older woman until the doubts about his
parentage are definitively put to rest. Oedipus, we can conclude, has
simply chosen to ignore a real possibility — that Polybus and Merope
are not his parents — a possibility he is demonstrably aware of. This
is not the kind of reasoning one expects from a Hellenic Sherlock
Holmes.

We know that Oedipus stayed away from Corinth because of his
dread of public ignominy, or his filial love for Polybus and Merope (or,

perhaps, a sexual attraction to Merope and a desire to avoid temptation and ensuing trouble with Polybus), or some combination of these or other reasons. Why, during his exile, he foolishly chose to ignore the possibility *which troubled him earlier and was not resolved by the oracle* — that Polybus and Merope were not his parents — and to tempt the fate that *had* been forecast by killing a man old enough to be his father and marrying a woman old enough to be his mother, we do not know.

The fourth puzzle Oedipus gives us in the very same speech. It concerns the identity of the gray-haired man in the carriage he attacked at "the place where three roads meet". Who was the feisty old man who swatted him on the head with a riding crop as he rode by after forcing him off the road?

> The one who led and the old man himself tried to drive me from the road by force. Then I, in anger, struck the one who was trying to push me aside, I mean the charioteer. The old man, when he saw this, watched for me going by the chariot and came down on me with his double whip on the middle of my head. He paid not merely an equal penalty, but with one decisive blow from the staff in this hand he was rolled backwards right out of the middle of his carriage; and I killed the lot of them.
> (OT 804-813)

While Oedipus is defending his macho pride, he is clearly *not* defending his life. The carriage was passing Oedipus when Laius, trying to vent a last drop of spleen, hit him on the head with a two-pronged riding crop. There is no suggestion that Laius planned to order his attendants to stop, turn back, and attack Oedipus. Oedipus simply retaliates in anger and starts killing. Like father, like son.

It might be said, on Oedipus' part, that no one caught up in a murderous rage is likely to do any investigating before striking. This may be true. But in the present circumstance pleading an unpremeditated "crime of passion" cannot be allowed. Oedipus had unresolved doubts about who his father really was. He had ample opportunity during his wandering exile from Corinth, between the day he received oracular advice in Delphi and the time he found himself at "the place where three roads meet", to consider in a cool-headed way what the upshot might be if in defense of his pride he were to get into a rage and kill a man old enough to be his father. Oedipus "measured" where

Corinth lay "by the stars". Consequently, at least one night separated his visit to the oracle from his encounter with Laius. But even if he had marched quickstep straightaway from oracle to crossroads, a man of truly superior intelligence who took the oracle's pronouncements seriously would, by the end of the first two kilometers, have figured out the possible consequences of killing a man old enough to be his father.

There are two further reasons to think that considerably more time than just a night passed between oracle and crossroads.

(a) The drunk insulted Oedipus. What did Oedipus do? Sat, silently took it, and went to his "parents" the next day to ask whether he really was their son. The members of Laius' group insulted and jostled Oedipus, and Laius swatted at him with a two-pronged stick. What did Oedipus do? *Killed them all (but one)!* What is the difference here? Age and self-confidence. The Oedipus who sat and took it was a very young man, a boy — the youth who, without seeking parental permission, went to consult the Delphic Oracle. The Oedipus who, in a macho rage, killed Laius and his men was a man whose wanderings in exile had strengthened and honed his physical prowess and given him self-assurance and courage.

(b) Because the Gulf of Corinth lies between Delphi and Corinth, to go *from* Delphi *to* Corinth, one travels southeast from Delphi toward the crossroads where the three roads meet. On hearing the oracle in Delphi, however, Oedipus fled *from Corinth*, not from Delphi. If Oedipus proceeded directly from the oracle to his fated encounter with Laius, he was actually fleeing from Corinth down the road *to* Corinth! This will not do! To go away from, to proceed in the opposite direction by land from Corinth, when one is in Delphi, one must travel *away* from the crossroads. Thus when Oedipus eventually did arrive at the crossroads, he was not coming *directly* from his session with the Delphic Oracle.

In any event, one would think that Oedipus would, when provoked, as he was by the peremptory and rude behavior of Laius and his henchmen, see Laius as a potential father, perhaps even spotting a bit of his own short fuse in the crotchety old man — if, that is, he really had the cleverness and intelligence he prides himself on having. Oedipus, we have already noted in this same speech, was capable of holding himself in check when angered:

I was angry and I barely restrained myself for that day.
(OT 781-82)

So far Oedipus has simply failed to show any interest in puzzles, or, when he does, any ability to put two and two together.

Oedipus' fifth and sixth, and most serious failures to undertake investigations, we learn about soon after the play begins, when Creon returns from Delphi with the oracle's command — although only later does it become clear how really odd it is that Oedipus did not make it his business early on to look into these matters: Oedipus did not investigate his predecessor's death or his wife-to-be's history, despite the oracle's warning and the uncertainty about his parentage that remained to be settled.

When Oedipus vanquished the Sphinx, he was clearly the hero of the day in Thebes. Laius, moreover, was not missing; he was known to be dead. There was a vacancy at the top. The Thebans were grateful and thought Oedipus had shown himself to be a man of excellence. Oedipus, on his part, doubtless felt an urge to put down roots after his wandering self-exile and to assume the power that he had earlier thought would be his in Corinth and was now clearly his for the asking in Thebes. The queen was a widow. Why should he not become ruler and further legitimize his power by marrying into the Theban royal family?

But did Oedipus at the time ask what had happened to Laius? When no one could tell him because the Sphinx had kept the citizens of Thebes too busy to permit them to carry out their own investigation into the circumstances of Laius' death, did the newly-crowned Oedipus then follow through by attempting to resolve the matter himself? He says that such an investigation *should* have been carried out:

> For even if the matter had not been pressed by a god, it was not fitting
> for you to leave it unpurified in this way, seeing that it was a great man
> and a king who had died, but it was fitting to search it out.
> (OT 255-58)

Right, Oedipus, by you, as well! As Oedipus soon points out, perhaps Laius was killed by Theban conspirators who may now wish him dead.

How, then, unless some intrigue, backed by money, was being worked
from this end, could the robber have proceeded to this level of daring?
(OT 124-25)

For it will not be on behalf of far-away friends, but for my own sake that
I shall dispel this pollution. Whoever it was that killed Laius might wish
to take vengeance on me with just such a murderous hand. Thus, in
defending him, I help myself.
(OT 137-41)

Despite the fact that he had excellent reasons to do so, Oedipus did not,
when he assumed the throne, bother to find out how and why his
predecessor had died.

Oedipus' failure to investigate this is underscored very pointedly
early in the play:

Creon. In this land, the god said. That which is sought can
be found, but that which is neglected escapes.
Oed.   Was it in the house, or in the countryside, or in
another country that Laius met this bloody death?
(OT 110-13)

Laius' widow, too, was old enough to be his mother. Did Oedipus
investigate her life before the wedding to assure himself he was not
marrying his mother? The oracle, after all, had not settled his doubts
concerning who his mother really was. No, Oedipus did not.

Oedipus has failed to ascertain the answers to six significant
questions that have clung to him since long before the plague arrived in
Thebes and remain still unresolved: (1) "Where did the scars on my
ankles come from?" (2) "Who are my real parents?" (3) "How can I
best avoid killing my father and marrying my mother?" (4) "Is this old
man who has forced me off the road and rudely swatted me from his
passing carriage my father?" (5) "Who killed the king whose throne I
have just been given?" (6) "Is this widow I am about to marry my
mother?" The more we learn by watching the plot unfold, when we
watch Oedipus' slowly trying to solve Laius' murder and his utter
failure to penetrate the riddles Teiresias sets him, the more it becomes
clear that, to put it gently, Oedipus' one intellectual success, his
solution of the riddle of the Sphinx, was a fluke. What we are told

about Oedipus' life clearly gainsays his reputation. He is not a prober and solver of mysteries. The pride he evinces when taunting Teiresias is drastically misplaced.

If, on the other hand, we ignore the fact that Oedipus has succeeded in laying a curse upon himself, and if we ignore further what Teiresias says about Oedipus having acted in ignorance:

> You have unknowingly been an enemy to your own kin below and on the
> earth above, . . .
>
> (OT 415-16)

there is an uncharitable interpretation: unlikely as it seems, after arriving in Thebes, defeating the Sphinx, and assuming power, Oedipus suspected or concluded that he had killed Laius and was marrying his mother, and all the cursing and public posturing we witness as the play progresses is designed to throw suspicion off himself and onto others.[21]

We find this interpretation unacceptable because (a) we take Teiresias to speak the truth about Oedipus acting in ignorance and (b) the interpretation requires that Oedipus be at the same time very smart and very stupid — smart to have acted so slyly in the past, all the while knowing the truth about himself, and stupid in acting as self-destructively as he clearly does during the course of the play.

If one rejects the uncharitable reading, these six mysteries in Oedipus' earlier life — six mysteries he was undoubtedly aware of, yet failed utterly to address or resolve — as well as his two intellectual failures displayed on stage, establish beyond doubt that he is not clever and has no real investigative genius to be proud of. In the first half of the play this conclusion receives another kind of support: Oedipus shows he has no respect for evidence. He pays attention to evidence only when it suits him.

When Teiresias is reluctant to reveal what he believes, Oedipus accuses him of being implicated in Laius' murder,

---

21. This, indeed, is almost the interpretation Vellacott puts forward in [1971].
   For further discussion of Vellacott's views, see the end of Part I.

> For know that you seem to me actually to have been a co-plotter of the deed, and to have done it, except in so far as killing him with your hands. If you happened to see, I should have said that this deed too was yours alone.
>
> (OT 346-49)

forgetting that he has just said,

> The man who had no fear when he was acting, words will not frighten him either.
>
> (OT 296)

This charge he makes on the basis of no evidence whatever, completely ignoring the point he had just made — that Teiresias would lie, not balk, if he were implicated in the murder.

Then, when Teiresias gets angry and does speak,

> I say that you are the killer of the man whose killer you seek.
>
> (OT 362)

> I say that unknowingly you have been living most shamefully with your nearest kin, and that you do not see the misfortune in which you are.
>
> (OT 366-67)

> Yes, and you are a foolish wretch to taunt me with these insults with which soon every man here will taunt you.
>
> (OT 372-73)

Oedipus accuses Creon, once again without a shred of evidence, of being the mastermind of Laius' murder, just because Creon went to the oracle and suggested that Teiresias be asked to help. Creon appears to defend himself and Oedipus says to him,

> You are skilled at speaking, but I am bad at taking lessons from you, for I have found you hostile and dangerous to me.
>
> (OT 545-46)

As Creon responds in his own defense:

If you believe that obstinacy without sense is a good possession, you are
not thinking wise.

(OT 549-50)

As proof of this, go to Delphi and ask if I reported the oracles truly to
you. Then next, if you catch me having planned anything together with
the soothsayer, take and kill me, not by a single but a double vote, mine
as well as your own. But do not accuse me solely on your own unclear
judgment. For it is not right without evidence to consider bad men good
or good men bad. [For I count casting off a good friend the same as
casting off one's own life, which one loves most.] But in time you will
come to know these things with certainty, since time alone shows a just
man, but you can come to know a bad man even in a single day.

(OT 603-15)

Later in the play, however, when Oedipus finally gets from Jocasta
a description of Laius' entourage and how he was travelling, Oedipus
begins to suspect that he was himself Laius' killer. Now he takes a
very great interest in evidence:

Cho. For us, indeed, O king, these things are a source of fear. Just the
       same, until you learn in full from the man who was there, have
       hope!
Oed. Yes, I have just this much hope, merely to wait for the herdsman.
Ioc. And when he has appeared, what do you want of him?
Oed. I will tell you. For if his account is found to be the same as yours,
       I at least will be cleared of disaster.
Ioc. What was out of the ordinary in the account you heard from me?
Oed. You said that he spoke of robbers as having killed Laius. Now if
       he is going to tell us the same number, I did not kill him; for one
       man could not be the same as the many. But if he speaks clearly
       of one man journeying alone, the guilt for this deed inclines
       towards me.

(OT 834-47)

Before concluding this section, let us engage, for a moment, in pure,
unbridled speculation. Oedipus' lone intellectual achievement is his
famous solution of the Sphinx's riddle.

Sphinx.   What is two-legged, three-legged, and four-legged?
Oed.   Man, who first crawls on all fours, then walks, and then uses a
            cane.

Did Oedipus get the answer right?

While Oedipus' answer may have been a welcome success, in that on hearing it the Sphinx self-destructed, it did not succeed because it was a *true* answer to the question the Sphinx asked.   Arms and canes are simply not legs.   If the Sphinx's question was: what is two-legged, three-legged, and four-legged? — the correct answer is: nothing.   The Sphinx did not ask: what *may appear* two-legged, three-legged, and four-legged?

Just as a distinguished bearded psychoanalytic authority may tell a patient all sorts of tales about how various parts of his psyche are acting, interacting, perhaps even warring, and succeed in effecting a cure — without truth being among the ingredients of the medicine he administers, so Oedipus delivered just the verbal blow the Sphinx was vulnerable to — without truth being a component of his weaponry.   The Sphinx was fooled into throwing herself off a mountain by a wrong answer that appeals to appearance.   To someone who doesn't know much about them, crawling babies may indeed *look* like they have four legs and people using canes like they have three.

Perhaps this is why Teiresias did not engage the Sphinx.   Who knows what someone who is willing to settle for appearances will take to be true?   As the saying goes,

Against stupidity even the gods themselves are powerless.

Oedipus has eyes and is gulled by appearances.   Teiresias has only his intellect.   When Oedipus taunts Teiresias about his failure to destroy the Sphinx and crows about his own success, Teiresias responds ironically with riddles,

I say, since you have taunted me specifically with my blindness: you
both have sight and do not see the misfortune you are in, nor where you
live, nor with whom you live.
(OT 412-14)

. . . [you], now seeing straight and true, but then darkness.
(OT 419)

I tell you: the man whom you have long been seeking, issuing threats
and proclaiming an inquiry into the murder of Laius, that man is here,
supposedly a stranger living among us, but in time he will be shown to
be a native Theban, and he will not rejoice in the turn of events. He who
had sight will be blind, and a beggar, who now is rich; pointing out the
ground to himself with his staff, he will journey to a foreign land. And
the same man will be found living as brother and father to his own
children, son and husband of the woman from whom he was born, and
to his father a sharer in his wife and a killer. Now go inside and think
on these things; and if you find that I have spoken falsely, consider
hereafter that I have no wisdom in prophecy.
(OT 449-62)

Indeed, the gist of these riddles should be nothing surprising to
Oedipus, who heard them years before in Delphi. He cannot claim that
they are new puzzles. Yet he was unable and is still unable to give
them true answers. Unlike the Sphinx's riddles, for Teiresias' riddles
answers that merely appeal to appearances will not work to banish the
plague from Thebes.

We do not wish to lay great (or for that matter any) weight upon the
speculation that Oedipus really failed to solve the riddle of the Sphinx.
The "logic" of riddles, readers may be tempted to object, *allows* —
indeed, calls for — solutions like the one Oedipus gave, answers that
are not literally true. The true and humdrum answer, "Nothing has
two, three, and four legs," just won't do! Perhaps. What is really important, what has been demonstrated beyond question, however, is that
Oedipus' answer to the Sphinx's riddle, true or not, was a lucky fluke
and anything but a product of great intellectual ability on his part.
Moreover, those who believe that non-literal solutions are legitimate to
riddles like the Sphinx's owe us some explanation of why non-literal
answers are not appropriate for the riddles Teiresias poses to Oedipus.

At the end, when Oedipus emerges blind and bleeding from the palace, is he finally Teiresias' equal? Has he gained Teiresias' insight? No, Oedipus still displays an obsession with public show. He persists in mistaking appearances, what light exposes and eyes see, for reality:

> For he tore the golden brooches from her robe, with which she was arrayed, and raised them and struck his own eyes in their sockets, saying such things as that they would not see the evils which he was suffering and doing, but from now on in darkness they would see those whom they should never have seen, and would not know those whom he wished to know.
>
> (OT 1268-74)

Oedipus is blind. He has learned the truth about his parricide and incest, although not through any cleverness on his part. Has he learned the general lesson: do not be concerned with appearances, reality is what counts? Has Oedipus really come to know himself?

Public Posturing

Oedipus' history shows very clearly that he has no keen, penetrating mind. The plot of *Oedipus Rex* is replete, however, with examples of Oedipus taking pride in, indeed, flaunting his supposed cleverness. And time and time again, Oedipus chooses to carry out his investigation before the public, when it could better, and for his own sake far more safely, be done in private.

As we have seen, the play begins with Oedipus appearing outside his palace to view first-hand the ravages of the plague and the suffering his subjects are undergoing. The priest-spokesman pleads with Oedipus to come to Thebes' rescue a second time. Oedipus informs the people gathered outside his palace that he has sent his brother-in-law, Creon, to the oracle at Delphi to seek advice.

Consider for a moment an alternative scenario in which Oedipus keeps the information about Creon's mission to himself. Suppose, for instance, Oedipus were to be prudent and limit his response to the priest to a promise to do his best to save Thebes from the plague — as once, long ago, he might add, he saved it from the Sphinx. What, indeed, does Oedipus gain by telling all Thebes that he has sent Creon to Delphi?

While a play consists, in great part, of dialogue, and dialogue consists, in great part, of exposing beliefs, *thought* as Aristotle puts it, in life much does remain private, even in the corridors of power. If Oedipus were wise, or at least concerned with the doubts we later learn he has, doubts that cast a great shadow over his life, he would be more cautious about what he says and does in public. He would play his cards closer to his vest. Of course, if Oedipus were prudent, or even restrained about letting anyone and everyone know what is on his mind and what he is up to, *Oedipus Rex* would be a very different play — in all likelihood a bad play, or at least an uninteresting one. It very soon becomes clear, however, that in Sophocles' play, Sophocles' Oedipus is a public posturer, far from secretive, prudent, or even self-contained.

Creon soon arrives from Delphi, and the second thing Oedipus hears from his mouth is:

> If you wish to hear with these people nearby, I am ready to speak, or I am ready to go within.
> (OT 91-92)

To his later detriment, of course, Oedipus reacts like a politician at election time:

> Tell it to all! The sorrow I feel for these people weighs with me more than even the concern for my own life.
> (OT 93-94)

Next, instead of getting on with the investigation called for by the oracle — probably because he has no idea how to begin a real one — Oedipus chooses once again to dance on tippy-toe before the public:

> To all you Cadmeans I proclaim this:
> (OT 223)

He condemns Laius' killer or killers, as well as anyone who has knowledge of the crime and keeps silent:

> I forbid this man, whoever he is, this land, whose power and throne I hold, and I forbid anyone to receive him or speak to him, or let him share in prayers or sacrifices to the gods, or to offer him a share in the holy water. And I command all to drive him from their homes, since this man is our pollution, as the Pythian oracle of the god has now revealed to me.
> (OT 236-43)

and goes on specifically to include himself, should he be found guilty — this before Teiresias has even appeared on stage to make his accusations. This kind of proclamation, threat, public bluster, and rhetoric is typical of politicians. To carry on a true investigation is not so easy.

By now the whole city (including, of course, any guilty parties it may hide) knows that the Delphic Oracle has made a prophecy, what the prophecy is, that an investigation of Laius' murder is to take place, and what will happen to the guilty party. Oedipus has needlessly, unwisely, and quite gratuitously boxed himself in. If he had received Creon in private and kept his investigation out of the public eye, then, when he discovered the truth, he could have stopped the plague by quietly leaving Thebes, with only a few people the wiser and no general opprobrium.

Nor does Oedipus have to let on to the public that he has sent for Teiresias. Nor does he have to receive Teiresias publicly. Teiresias himself wants nothing to do with public appearances and makes no bones about it:

> I do not speak because I see that, in your case, your words do not go to
> the mark; so I'm seeing that I do not make the same mistake.
> (OT 324-25)

By receiving Teiresias in public, and insulting, angering, and prodding him until he speaks, Oedipus publicly bears the blunt of the terrible words Teiresias finally utters — with the result that, in a reckless and ill-natured act of face-saving, Oedipus publicly accuses Teiresias and then Creon of Laius' murder. Then, naturally, Teiresias and Creon feel obliged in turn to defend themselves publicly.

Jocasta has the right idea:

> Foolish men, why have you raised this pointless verbal strife? Are you
> not ashamed, while the land is sick in this way, to stir up your private
> troubles? Go into the palace, and you Creon, go to your house! And
> don't make a trifling matter into a big grief!
> (OT 634-38)

The chorus chimes in with good advice, which, if followed, might have kept the truth about Oedipus from becoming public knowledge:

Lady, why do you delay to take him [Oedipus] into the house?
                    (OT 678)

Had Oedipus allowed Jocasta to do this, he might have made the discovery in private that he murdered Laius and been able to leave Thebes without attendant fanfare, or with the Corinthians' new offer as an excuse.

The Corinthian messenger attempts to be discreet:

Oed.   A terrible oracle, stranger, sent upon us by the gods.
Mess.   Can it be told? Or is it not right for another to know?
Oed.   Assuredly it is.
                    (OT 992-94)

Oedipus, characteristically, will have none of discretion.

Finally, when at play's end Creon enters and confronts the now-blind Oedipus, his first thought is to get Oedipus inside, away from the public gaze:

But if you no longer respect the generations of men, at least revere the all-nurturing flame of our lord the Sun, by not showing him thus unveiled a pollution such as this that neither earth nor holy rain nor light will welcome. Quick as you can, take him into the house! For it is right for kin alone to see, for kin alone to hear the troubles in the family.
                    (OT 1424-31)

Oedipus does not go in, but remains outside surrounded by morbidly curious onlookers, begging that his wife be buried properly and that his daughters be looked after. Creon once again says:

The point you have reached in your weeping is far enough! Go inside the house!
                    (OT 1515)

Still Oedipus stays put to argue with Creon that he should be sent into exile. Creon repeats for the third time:

Go, then, but let go of the children!
> (OT 1521)

Finally, Creon has to order his attendants to take Oedipus away into the palace. Oedipus, it seems — blinded, reputation shattered — still cannot get enough of the public.

Only once in the play does Oedipus express the slightest misgiving about pursuing business publicly:

I fear, lady, that I have spoken far too many words, and so I wish to see him [the herdsman].
> (OT 767-68)

But having aired this wee glitch of a doubt and put it behind him, Oedipus plunges ahead in typical fashion.

We have seen in the preceding chapter how the characters of *Oedipus Rex* air in dialogue what they know of Oedipus' history and in so doing give proof that the genius on which he prides himself is non-existent. The actions of the plot further support this conclusion by showing that Oedipus has no genuine respect for evidence or fact. The present chapter, too, provides additional corroboration from the plot that keen intellect is not one of Oedipus' gifts. The clever man in Oedipus' position would exercise prudence and be cautious about what he says and does in public, instead of seizing center-stage at every possible opportunity in order to gain plaudits for himself and flaunt his supposed intellect.

Character Flaws

The details cited in the preceding section definitely establish that Oedipus is not a private person. Oedipus is king, an exceptionally public king, driven, even to the point of foolishness, to seek out and bathe in the limelight. He prizes recognition and adulation. Indeed, it may have been his love for kudos and public posturing that brought him to Thebes to challenge the Sphinx in the first place.

As the action unfolds, we see this love of public recognition and adulation manifest itself in large part as an arrogant confidence and false pride in his "genius", his own vaunted intellectual ability. In his confrontation with Teiresias Oedipus revels in the fact that he solved the riddle of the Sphinx and Teiresias did not. He is proud of his supposed ability to solve mysteries. But as the play progresses, an overwhelming body of evidence builds up which establishes that Oedipus has no talent for investigation to be proud of or arrogant about at all — even, perhaps, in his defeat of the Sphinx.

Not only does Oedipus have a large ego which thirsts for praise and renown, he is extremely defensive, aggressively so, when he feels himself or his reputation the least threatened. As we watch he springs to the defense of his good name by mounting a sudden irrational attack on first Teiresias and then Creon.

For years Oedipus has balanced on razor's edge. Early on, the whole tenor of his life and reputation was shaken by the oracle's prophecy. Although the oracle in no way resolved the uncertainty about who his parents were that led him to consult it in the first place, his obsession with recognition and glory pressed him to seek out public life. He could not stand to become an anonymous, private person. Public life is where reputations are enhanced. But the higher one soars, the more the risk, and the greater distance there is to fall. Oedipus is a man driven to live at risk.

Worse yet, Oedipus' temper has a hair trigger. As Teiresias observes,

> *Teir.* You fault my temper, yet you have not seen your own which lives close to you, but you rebuke me.
> *Oed.* Well, who would not be angry upon hearing the kind of words with which you now slight our city?
> (OT 337-40)

The trait Teiresias is accusing Oedipus of living close to is anger. We ourselves see his temper flare in his interchanges with Teiresias and Creon. But to Teiresias Oedipus *lives close to* anger. Indeed, after an initial jostle by Laius' charioteer, a goodbye tap on the head from the passing Laius is a final insult that angers Oedipus enough to kill five of the six men in Laius' party. Oedipus should, of course, know better. He had ample time to realize that the oracle did not resolve his doubts concerning his parents. The old man in the chariot might indeed be his father.

Thus far: Oedipus has a mistaken pride in his investigative skills, loves to bask in the limelight, and has a great ego that thirsts for public life and acclaim. At times he carries this obsession to the point of foolishness. He is extremely defensive when he perceives a threat to himself or his reputation and has a hair-trigger temper. In summary: Oedipus is an unintelligent macho posturer.

To say this of a man in the modern world of the 1990s is to condemn him. But in the world of ancient Greece — where the word "modest" had no favorable synonym, and almost all work was done by women and slaves, while the free male citizens did the governing, occasional warring, and carrying out of vendettas — to be judged a macho posturer was probably no insult, although to be judged a dumb macho posturer who thinks himself clever and takes things unnecessarily to the point of foolishness doubtless was. Even the chorus remarks, during the interchange between Oedipus and Teiresias,

We do not need such angry words, but how best we shall accomplish the god's oracles, this we must consider.

(OT 406-07)

Oedipus, we learn, has two other negative characteristics: disloyalty and lack of honesty toward those closest to him.

Disloyalty. By his own account, Creon is his friend.

. . . how great is the envy which keeps watch under your roof, if for the sake of this power which the state put in my hands, given to me but not sought, Creon the loyal, Creon the original friend, has come upon me by stealth and desires to drive me out . . .

(OT 382-86)

It was Creon Oedipus sent to consult the oracle. Yet when Teiresias finally accuses him of being Laius' killer, Oedipus, with arrogant self-assurance and no evidence at all, charges Creon with masterminding the murder and plotting to take Oedipus' throne. This is not loyalty to one's friend and brother-in-law. Indeed, after a mere three-plus more pages of dialogue between Oedipus and Creon, Oedipus tells Creon:

No, not at all! I wish you dead, not banished.

(OT 623)

Later, when Jocasta realizes that Oedipus is Laius' murderer and her own son, she tries to dissuade him from pursuing his "investigations" further. Immediately Oedipus turns on her and publicly accuses her of fearing that people will find out she has married below her station:

Don't worry! For even if I am shown to be the son of a slave mother, from a line of slaves, you will not be proved to be of low birth.

(OT 1062-63)

This is not the kind of loyalty we expect from a husband for his wife.

Creon and Jocasta, Oedipus' friend and his wife, are the only adults we meet who are in any way close to him. Yet, gratuitously and without evidence, he accuses the one of murder and treason and the other of caring mainly about her social status. Oedipus is disloyal to wife and friend. Oedipus is not a nice man.

Another flaw in Oedipus' character is his lack of honesty with the person closest to him, his wife. This is seen not in the events of the plot, but in the dialogue as Oedipus' history is revealed. In his pursuit of power in Thebes, Oedipus comes to Jocasta aware that a cloud hangs over him which may touch her as well. Oedipus has not had his uncertainty about his parentage resolved; but he *has* been warned by the Delphic Oracle that he will marry his mother. Oedipus' failure to disclose this is comparable to the failure of a man who suspects he may have a venereal disease to tell his fiancee because he fears he will lose the chance to gain her family's wealth and status. The least Oedipus could have done was to let Jocasta know what the oracle had and had not said. If Oedipus had been the slightest bit candid, and he and Jocasta had been able to compare oracular predictions, the further disaster of their marriage might well have been averted.

Some Answers to Earlier Questions

We are now in the position to answer the questions raised about *Oedipus Rex* in the beginning:

Why is Oedipus, to all appearances the best solver of mysteries in Thebes, the last major character in *Oedipus Rex* to realize the truth?

Because Oedipus has no talent whatever for solving mysteries. Oedipus' defeat of the Sphinx was at best a fluke. Indeed, he may not even have got the right answer to the riddle — although he definitely did get lucky, in that the answer he gave, right or wrong, the Sphinx took to be right, and this provoked its destruction.

What actually happens in the plot of Oedipus Rex? What great fallibilities are displayed by Oedipus in the actions dramatized on stage that lead to the drastic change in his fortunes?

King Oedipus, because he is arrogantly proud of an intellectual genius he mistakenly believes himself to have, because he is obsessed with being in the public eye and gaining plaudits for himself, and because of his sheer foolishness in thinking that doing so will add to his reputation, chooses to make public that an investigation into the murder of his predecessor, Laius, is needed to defeat the plague which has fallen upon Thebes, to undertake that investigation himself, and to carry out all phases of it in public. Unbeknownst to him, although not so unknown as to be an utter surprise, the truth is that he is Laius' son, he has stupidly let himself murder his father, and he has stupidly married and fathered children upon his own mother, and has done so in arrogant pursuit of status and power without disclosing to her the shadow that hangs over him. Each time people try to shield him from this truth, parts of which bubble to the surface again and again in various forms as the play unfolds, he loses his temper, becomes angry, defensive, and lashes out with ill-founded and completely false accusations against them: that Teiresias, the blind prophet, is a fake who is spreading slander to hide his own complicity in Laius' murder, that Creon, his brother-in-law and friend, masterminded Laius' death and now conspires to overthrow Oedipus himself, and that Jocasta, his wife, is more concerned about her social status and reputation than with his problems. When the truth finally outs, Jocasta hangs herself, and Oedipus puts out his eyes.

Is Oedipus simply a victim of his fate, or, given the kind of person he is shown to be as the play progresses, is it reasonable to think that the part he plays in bringing about his own downfall is more than merely passive, and that the smarter of the gods — Apollo, for instance — might well have predicted, rather than pre-ordained it?

Oedipus himself is of two minds about this question. He says first

No mortal except me can bear my ills.
(OT 1414-15)

and seems to take the responsibility and guilt. Yet later he says to Creon:

Then may you be happy, and for bringing them [sc. my daughters] here may god turn out to guard you better than me!
(OT 1478-79)

implying that it was bad luck that brought him where he is and not deeds over which he was himself responsible. Apollo and not himself he accuses of bringing about his downfall:

It was Apollo, friends, Apollo, who was bringing my ills, my ills, my sorrows, to fulfilment. But the hand that struck my eyes was none but my own, to my sorrow.
(OT 1329-32)

Certainly the gods brought Oedipus and Laius together at the place where the three roads meet. But Oedipus has only himself to blame for losing his temper at the swat of a man old enough to be his father. He had had plenty of time beforehand to muse about the implications of the oracle's prophecy and the still unsettled doubt about who his parents were.[22] And perhaps it was the gods who brought him to Thebes and not his own drive to win renown and public acclaim. But no one else but he became arrogant about his "accomplishment" of answering the Sphinx's riddle "correctly". No one else but he sought status by putting himself on Laius' throne without investigating Laius' murder, or by marrying a widowed queen old enough to be his mother without putting to rest, once and for all, the uncertainty about his parentage, or sharing his doubts and history with her. Finally, it was his foolish preoccupation with bringing still further honors upon himself and his false pride in his intellectual "genius" that made him carry out an investigation of Laius' murder publicly before the eyes of everyone in Thebes. Oedipus, although he still seems not to have gained the wisdom to realize it even at play's end, cannot legitimately shift the blame for his suffering away from himself and onto the gods, fate, or ill fortune.

Later, in *Oedipus at Colonus*, Oedipus refuses to support his son, Polyneices, and his son's allies from Argos in their planned invasion of Thebes, and instead curses both his sons, saying that they will slay each other and Polyneices' forces from Argos will be defeated. Polyneices believes Oedipus' words will be realized.

---

22. There is a theological issue here in which we do not wish to become entangled. Some argue that all human actions are predestined by God or the gods and that, still, humans are at times *also* responsible for what they do. Others argue that if the gods predestine all human actions, humans bear no moral responsibility for what they do. We wish to sidestep this controversy. The principal issue is that of whether Oedipus bears some moral responsibility for the two terrible events of his life — killing his father and marrying his mothers. We claim that he does. He was aware that there was doubt about his parentage. This doubt was not put to rest by the Delphic Oracle. He had time to reflect on this fact before he slew Laius and married Jocasta. So when we say that Oedipus has *only* himself to blame for certain events, we ask those readers who believe, as did some ancient Greeks, that the gods predestine all human affairs to take us as accepting that the gods are responsible and then going on to say that Oedipus *was morally culpable for these events as well.*

> *Ant.*   Then do you see how you are bringing his prophecies to pass, who
> speaks of death for the two of you at each other's hands?
> (OC 1424-25)

> *Pol.*   Yes, and do not restrain me! This path will now be my concern,
> with evil doom and suffering from my father here and from his
> Furies. May Zeus grant you both prosperity, if you do these things
> for me! Now let me go, and farewell! For never again will you
> see me living!
> (OC 1432-38)

Polyneices believes Oedipus' prediction; he believes he is doomed. Yet
he answers that he will not call off his attack on Thebes. He will carry
on as before even towards his death. In no way, however, is it Polyneices' view that Oedipus has predestined or is causing him to carry on,
attack Thebes, and die.

Similarly, Apollo has predicted Oedipus' fate correctly and Oedipus
now believes it, but he has no more grounds for thinking Apollo has
caused him to kill Laius and marry Jocasta than Polyneices has for
thinking Oedipus is causing him to attack Thebes and kill, and be killed
by, his brother.

Other Views

Much has been written about *Oedipus Rex*. Let us end this discussion by comparing the view set out in the preceding sections to those of other recent commentators. These remarks will fall under three headings: (A) elements of Oedipus' character, (B) events in the story that some find odd or in need of explanation, and (C) the ("uncharitable") interpretation of Philip Vellacott.

(A) On the view of *Oedipus Rex* just set out, much that happens in the story springs from four major traits Oedipus displays in the events enacted or spoken about on stage:

(1) He is foolishly obsessed with being in the public eye and winning renown for himself.

(2) He has no talent at all for solving mysteries, but takes pride in having one.

(3) He is extraordinarily and irrationally defensive when he believes himself or his reputation under attack.

(4) He has a trigger temper.

Concerning (4), when the question is whether Oedipus does at times act in fits of sudden, hot-blooded anger, commentators unanimously agree. He does. As to (3), some identify Oedipus' attacks on Teiresias, Creon, and Jocasta as defensiveness (or hot temper) and others, surprisingly, do not. As to (2), we said in the Introduction that much written about *Oedipus Rex* is not merely wrong, but 180 degrees wrong. To our knowledge *no other interpreters* have argued that Oedipus entirely lacks a keen intellect and that his defeat of the Sphinx was at best a lucky fluke. On the contrary, almost all commentators see Oedipus as possessing a keen and powerful mind. And finally, no one else,

47

so far as we know, has even suggested that Oedipus had the characteristic mentioned in (1).

Let us begin there. The chorus is a permanent fixture in the plays of Sophocles and his predecessors.[23] So in one sense, tradition and convention dictate that what goes on on stage goes on before a stage public. But surely we do not wish to be committed to the idea that the character flaw of being foolishly obsessed with reputation and winning renown for oneself cannot be treated in Greek theater because custom dictates that protagonists nearly always appear in company of a chorus. Furthermore, the observation that the plot of a play about a more sensible and private Oedipus would not be a good plot, or a Greek plot — even if we grant its truth — does not refute the contention that Sophocles' *Oedipus Rex* is obsessed with appearing in public and gaining plaudits for himself, that he is, in short, an unintelligent macho posturer, and that he would do far better by carrying out whatever investigations circumstances require discreetly and in private.

But Oedipus is King. Save for the final scene, the entire play amounts to a series of royal audiences with King Oedipus' subjects present and attentive. Oedipus insists on doing his business in public, despite the fact that Creon, Teiresias, Jocasta, the Corinthian messenger, and the survivor-herdsman all indicate one way or another that business need not be done this way and might better proceed out of the public eye.

And in the final scene — although it is definitely not a royal audience of King Oedipus — Oedipus insists on remaining before the public even when he is urged three times not to. Ultimately he has to be forced into the privacy of his home.

That all scenes of the play but the last consist of Oedipus' royal audiences explains several of the items which fall under (B). It has troubled some commentators that characters in the play insist on telling each other things they must already know. Oedipus, however, appears in his persona as King. When he addresses Creon and the other major

---

23. Well, almost. Both *Antigone* and *Oedipus at Colonus* contain scenes in which no chorus is present. In *Oedipus Rex*, however, the chorus is present throughout.

figures in the play and when they address him, all of them aim their speeches also at the Court, the assembled subjects who cannot be assumed to know what is being talked about. The major personages speak formally and publicly, even in the last scene, which is Creon's first audience as leader. Thus we cannot agree with those commentators who cite, as stage conventions or weaknesses in the construction of the play, examples in which major characters state what they know their principal addressees already know:

> Just as Sophocles anticipated our unvoiced objection that it was unlikely that Oedipus would know nothing of the plague . . . so here the arrival of Creon is prepared by having Oedipus say that he is surprised he is not here already. We are disarmed by the transparent honesty with which Sophocles avails himself of accepted stage convention to overcome certain improbabilities. If we were not so disarmed, we might fret over the sequence of improbabilities that follows. To put the audience in full possession of the facts Sophocles makes Creon tell Oedipus a number of things which Oedipus must have known already. "We had a king once called Laius" says Creon (103). "I've heard of him. Never actually saw him of course" replies Oedipus. Dramatic irony certainly, but at a price. (Dawe [1982], p. 8.)

Oedipus doubtless does know these things already, but his subjects in attendance may not themselves know or know that he knows. Sophocles, therefore, makes him and Creon converse formally and let those in *their* audience in on what they know.

Dawe goes on to draw attention to the speeches between 765 and 860 in which Oedipus troubles to inform his wife of many years that his father was Polybus of Corinth and his mother the Dorian Merope ([1982], p. 17).

Jocasta, of course, does know who Oedipus thinks his parents are, but again the other people who are on stage and listening may well not.

> In this last comment, Aristotle indicates a trait which is certainly open to criticism — the ignorance of Oedipus as to the story of Laius . . . he does not know whether this had befallen him at Thebes, or in its neighbourhood, or abroad (109-113). Nor does he know that Laius was reported to have been slain by robbers, and that only one of his followers had escaped (116-123): and he asks if no search had been made at the time (128, 566). Iocasta, who has now been his wife for many years,

tells him, as if for the first time, the story of the oracle given to Laius,
and he tells her the story of his own early fortunes . . . Still it is evident
that the measure of past reticence imagined, both on their part and on his,
exceeds the limit of verisimilitude. The true defence of this improbability
consists in frankly recognising it. Exquisite as was the dramatic art
exercised within the scope of the action (ἐν τοῖς πράγμασι), this art was
still so far naive as to feel no offence at some degree of freedom in the
treatment of that which did not come within the framework, — of that
which, in Aristotle's phrase, lay "outside the piece". (Jebb [1966], pp.
xv-xxvi.)

Again, Oedipus is not speaking *merely* to Jocasta, or Jocasta to him.

To return now to (2), Oedipus' lack of the intellectual talent he
mistakenly prides himself for having, and, indeed, (3), his irrational
defensiveness, Bernard Knox's reading of the play differs most radically
from the one documented and argued for here:

[Oedipus] is a great man, a man of experience and swift courageous
action, who yet acts only after careful deliberation, illuminated by an
analytic and demanding intelligence. His action by its consistent success
generates a great self-confidence, but it is always directed to the common
good. He is an absolute ruler who loves and is loved by his people, but
is conscious of the jealousy his success arouses and suspicious of
conspiracy in high places. (Knox [1957], p. 29.)

We have not been able to find a single occasion where Oedipus "acts
only after careful deliberation, illuminated by an analytic and
demanding intelligence". Oedipus' action on stage is almost always
directed by his desire for public recognition, not for "the common
good". Although a person's action may be directed both by a desire for
public plaudits and for the common good, there is evidence in Oedipus'
case that the first desire is operative, since he insists on pursuing things
in public even when many others indicate that they might best be
handled in private. How much credible evidence is there that the
common good ranks high on the list of his priorities? And in whom
does his success arouse jealousy?

The decisive actions are the product of an admirable character; with the
possible exception of his anger (and even that springs initially from his

devotion to the city) their source is the greatness and nobility of the man and the ruler. (Knox [1957], p. 31.)

What does poor Creon do to provoke, much less merit his anger and Jocasta his scorn? How is impugning the characters of Creon and Jocasta something admirable, noble, or great? And doing it in public?

> Oedipus did have one freedom: he was free to find out or not find out the truth . . . the freedom to search for the truth, the truth about the prophecies, about the gods, about himself. And of this freedom he makes full use. Against the advice and appeals of others, he pushes on, searching for the truth, the whole truth and nothing but the truth. And in this search he shows all those great qualities . . . courage, intelligence, perseverance, the qualities that make human beings great. This freedom to search, and the heroic way in which Oedipus uses it, make the play not a picture of man's utter feebleness caught in the toils of fate, but on the contrary, a heroic example of man's dedication to the search for truth, the truth about himself. (Knox in Fagles [1984], pp. 134-135.)

Surely Oedipus was free to carry on the investigation out of the public eye. He could meet with the surviving eye-witness to Laius' death in private. He certainly does not put his freedom to investigate to much sensible use. He is definitely not interested in the whole truth and nothing but it. He does not bother to find out the truth to the many puzzles of his life. He is not interested in doing any real investigating into the supposed plot of Creon and Teiresias. And he shows very little intelligence.

As to the matter of Oedipus' intellectual skills, here is a further survey of opinion — all of it, if our analysis is correct, completely wide of the mark. We shall not bother to respond to every quotation by repeating observations and arguments already set down.

> Whether there is a "tragic flaw", a *hamartia*, in King Oedipus is uncertain, though I doubt it, as he is hardly a figure who shoots wide of the mark. Accuracy is implicit in his nature. (Bloom [1988], p. 1)

> To protest Apollo is necessarily dialectical, since the pride and agility of the intellect of Oedipus, remorselessly searching out the truth, in some sense is also Apollo's. (Bloom [1988], p. 4)

. . . Teiresias arrives, and is greeted in terms of extreme reverence. Oedipus, the most brilliant of men, greets the prophet with humility and trust. (Dawe [1982], p. 10)

The essence of the matter is this: the apparent failure of the highly intelligent Oedipus to grasp what has been said to him is unconvincing . . . the apparent failure of Oedipus at the time to grasp what is being said to him, we can do no more than admit that it is so, adding that Greek tragedy at large teems with examples of inconsistency of character, and that actors of great professional skill can get away with almost anything. (Dawe [1982], p. 12)

Oedipus is a "good king", a father of his people, an honest and great ruler, while at the same time an outstanding intellect. (Ehrenberg [1968], p. 74)

The foundations of his life have gone, but his great and powerful mind knows of no despair. He still relies on his own genius, and it is indeed the very core of his tragedy that, by using his high intellect honestly and uncompromisingly, he brings doom upon himself. (Ehrenberg [1968], p. 77)

Characteristic of his intelligence is his insistence on complete knowledge and clarity. He demands a rational foundation for his existence: he admits no mysteries, no half-truths, no half-measures. (Knox [1957], p. 18)

Wow! Why the scars? Who are my parents? Who is this old man? Whom am I marrying? Did the Oracle really say what Creon says it did?

His is a sharply critical intelligence . . . creative too. It can not only ask questions: it can answer them. And Oedipus' fame and reputation is based above all on his solution of the riddle of the Sphinx. (Knox [1957], pp. 19-20)

The man whose intelligent and courageous action made him the envy of his fellow men will not accept a life based on willed ignorance; he cannot inhabit a world of uncertainties but must re-establish the intellectual clarity in which he has always existed. (Knox [1957], p. 31)

Regarding his parentage? Regarding the scars? Regarding the old man in the carriage? Regarding the woman he is marrying? Regarding Teiresias and Creon's alleged plot? The *only* intellectual success *in his whole life* that Oedipus has to boast about is his defeat of the Sphinx.

(B) Some commentators have found certain features of *Oedipus Rex* odd or in need of explanation. One such point has already been mentioned: at times one character will give another information when the former is aware the latter already knows it. There are four further issues, concerning (i) the oracle Oedipus once heard at Delphi, (ii) Oedipus' scars, (iii) Teiresias' prophetic ability, and (iv) the story told by the servant-herdsman who survived the massacre of Laius' entourage. (i) and (iv) will be treated under this heading. (ii) and (iii) will be incorporated into the discussion of Vellacott's interpretation (C).

(i) How Oedipus reacted to what the Delphic Oracle did and did not say:

> Could not Oedipus . . . have escaped his doom if he had been more careful? Knowing that he was in danger of committing parricide and incest, would not a really prudent man have avoided quarrelling, even in self-defence, with men older than himself, and also love-relations with women older than himself? Would he not, in Waldock's ironic phrase, have compiled a handlist of all the things he must not do? In real life I suppose he might. But we are not entitled to blame Oedipus either for carelessness in failing to compile a handlist or for lack of self-control in failing to obey its injunctions. For no such possibilities are mentioned in the play, or even hinted at; and it is an essential critical principle that *what is not in the play does not exist.* (Dodds [1988], p. 39)

Dodds is wrong. In the play there definitely are the possibilities he mentions. Oedipus says he went to Delphi to get an answer to the question of whether Polybus and Merope were his parents because he was not sure whether they were; and he also says that he did not get an answer when he asked the oracle this question. Therefore, a handlist of do's and do-not's is quite appropriate, given that he values his reputation and does not wish to kill his father and marry his mother. In such circumstances, a man *would* avoid quarrelling violently with a man old enough to be his father, especially when his life is in *no* way threatened, and marrying a woman old enough to be his mother — *if* he were truly prudent *and intelligent.*

> In any case, Sophocles has provided a conclusive answer to those who suggest that Oedipus could, and therefore should, have avoided his fate. The oracle was *unconditional* (l. 790): it did not say "If you do so-and-so you will kill your father"; it simply said "You will kill your father, you will sleep with your mother". And what an oracle predicts is bound to happen. Oedipus does what he can to evade his destiny: he resolves never to see his supposed parents again. (Dodds [1988], p. 39)

Again, even granting the infallibility of oracles, Oedipus obviously did not throw up his hands and return to Corinth. He *tried* to escape his destiny. And if he had a truly creative intelligence, he might have considered many other ways of attempting to do so. He had consulted the oracle because there was some question in his mind about whether Polybus and Merope were his parents. In the passages above, Dodds passes over the fact that the oracle did not answer the key question Oedipus asked it: who his parents really were. There are many strategies a man might employ in an attempt to avoid killing his father, marrying his mother, and thereby ruining his reputation. A cautionary handlist is one, immediate suicide another.

(iv) The story of the servant-herdsman.

Dawe draws attention to a conflict in this story which "defies the logic and probabilities of real life" ([1982], p. 16). Jocasta's knowledge of Laius' death comes from what the herdsman told her at their interview. She says that the herdsman reported to her immediately upon his return to Thebes, *when Oedipus was already king.* Yet how is it that the herdsman, "running for his life," does not get to Thebes before Oedipus? Dawe lays this down to a "telescoping of time . . . perfectly familiar in Greek Tragedy" ([1982], p. 16).

There is indeed a point of conflict here. Early in the play, Creon definitely implies that the survivor arrived in Thebes *before* Oedipus. On arrival he was interrogated by Creon and other Theban leaders about Laius' death. But the investigation was cursory because Oedipus had not yet appeared to kill the Sphinx and Creon and the others viewed the threat then posed by the Sphinx as paramount and demanding their full attention. After testifying before them that a band of robbers attacked Laius' entourage — exaggerating, no doubt, to avoid the telling admission that he and the rest of Laius' attendants failed to protect their king from the attack of one lone man — he went about his business. Then, suddenly, a foreigner showed up, conquered the Sphinx, and, naturally, became everybody's hero. Is this slave, when he first catches a glimpse of the Great Man, who by this time has been made king and is married to Laius' queen, going to come forward and accuse him of an unspeakable crime — admitting in the process that he perjured himself in his earlier testimony by exaggerating the odds against which he fought and failed? No.

Later in the play, however, Jocasta seems to say that the survivor arrived *after* Oedipus had assumed the throne.

> As soon as he came back from there and saw that you held power and Laius was dead, he touched my hand and supplicated me to send him to the fields and to the pastures of the flocks, so that he might be as far as possible from the sight of this town.
>
> (OT 758-62)

There is conflict only if one reads this passage as implying that the time the survivor got back *was* the time he saw how things were and came to beg Jocasta to send him to the mountains. Even so, Jocasta may simply have taken it for granted that the survivor came directly to her upon his return, when in fact he had not. Indeed, the survivor may have misled her on the point; we know he strayed from the truth when testifying earlier about the circumstances of Laius' death.

Vellacott finds another difficulty[24]. Early in the play, when Creon tells Oedipus how Laius died, he mentions that one of Laius' attendants survived the massacre and returned to Thebes. Oedipus straightaway undertakes an investigation, yet does not send for this eye-witness. Later, Oedipus himself mentions the witness, but still does not send for him. Only when the play is half-over does Oedipus finally summon the man. Why?

---

24. Vellacott, [1971], p. 115.

The answer to Vellacott's "Why?" is that: First, Oedipus is not very smart. Second, his attention is on posturing and the proclamation he is about to make which promises rewards to those who come forward to help his investigation and severe punishments to those who fail to do so. Third, when he finishes this performance, Teiresias appears and further distracts him. Finally, it is only when the testimony of the survivor becomes necessary to the defense *of his own reputation* that he sees to it that the man is summoned.

(C) Vellacott's own interpretation is of special interest because it qualifies among those we have labelled "uncharitable": Oedipus in marrying Jocasta *suspected or knew what he was doing.*

According to Vellacott, Oedipus is a man with two sides, one a public face he puts on for others, the second the secret man inside he knows or strongly suspects himself to be.

The public Oedipus is the son of Polybus and Merope, King and Queen of Corinth. His conscience is clear. He has exiled himself from Corinth because of the terrible prophecy given him in Delphi in his youth. He killed the men at the crossroads in response to their vicious attack upon him. Like the rest of his subjects, he believes that Laius died at the hands of thieves or unknown enemies in Thebes. He takes it for granted that marrying Laius widow upon his succession to the throne was perfectly proper.

The secret inner Oedipus is the one who as a young man began to have doubts about his parentage. He suppressed his suspicions when he heard the oracle and fled from Corinth. They remained suppressed until he arrived in Thebes. Laius was not long dead and speculations about his death were doubtless on the lips of everyone. Oedipus *must* have connected what he heard about the murder of Laius and his attendants to his own bloody deeds not long before. He could not have forgotten the oracle's prediction either: that he would kill his father and marry his mother. How, with marriage on the horizon, could he miss connecting the killing he had done with the killing the oracle spoke of? There is also another, final connection: that since the king he killed was almost certainly his father, that king's widow, the woman he was about to marry, was probably his mother. Having realized this not long after setting foot in Thebes, why, then, does he risk getting married to Jocasta? "Ambition, backed by courage, with only a thin thread of excuse, namely that his relationship to Iocasta was . . . a strong probability rather than a certainty," answers Vellacott[25].

Having come to know this, or at least suspect it, Oedipus tries throughout the years that follow to atone for his guilt by being a good king, husband, and father. But the plague puts an end to it all. The conditions for putting an end to the plague are laid down by the oracle: expose and banish or kill Laius' murderer. To save Thebes, Oedipus knowingly sets in train his own exposure as Laius' killer. But it is not required and not part of his plan that he expose the fact that he has secretly known of his guilt all along.[26]

To repeat our earlier criticisms of this kind of interpretation: First, Teiresias says that Oedipus committed the terrible deeds — including his incestuous marriage — *in ignorance*, and when Teiresias does speak in his role as seer, he is a man to be believed. Secondly, this interpretation demands that Oedipus be both more intelligent and less intelligent than he shows himself to be.

If Oedipus really were as intelligent and perceptive as Vellacott makes him out, why did he choose to exile himself from Corinth? While his suspicion that he had killed his father and married his mother might cause him to suppress "the knowledge that Polybus was probably not his father"[27], why should he have suppressed this supposed knowledge way back at the time he consulted the oracle? Again, why should he stupidly decide that there was "only one way to save Thebes"[28] — that is, to lead others, by hook and crook, to discover the truth "as it were by accident"[29]? Why not simply confess, or commit suicide leaving a note? Why not simply vanish — leave Thebes quietly and

---

25. [1971], p. 118.

26. See Vellacott [1971], pp. 119-120.

27. *Ibid.*

28. *Ibid.*

29. *Ibid.*

disappear, thus banishing the killer of Laius, saving Thebes from the plague, and at the same time leaving behind a mystery instead of a tarnished reputation? Or why should not Oedipus tell Creon and Jocasta that he was exiling himself as the oracle directed because he had discovered his involvement in Laius' death — without letting anyone else know and without letting them know his true parentage?

Lack of compelling answers to questions like these shows that Vellacott's reading cannot be sustained as a plausible interpretation of the story. But before leaving Vellacott to move on, however, we shall touch briefly upon his views concerning the two topics that remain from (B): Oedipus' scars and Teiresias' prophetic ability.

(ii)   Oedipus' scars.

Vellacott suggests that the young Oedipus began to have suspicions about his parentage because of the "malformation", the "terrible reproach", of his feet.[30]

> . . . if foot-piercing were a traditional practice, however rare, the scars would mean that Oedipus grew up knowing he was a foundling. As it is, the orthodox view of the play has to insist that Oedipus, even after being told by the drunken guest that he was not Polybus' son, even after being refused enlightenment by Polybus, and even after being given at Delphi a prophecy which suggested something mysterious in his relationship with his parents, still did not think of connecting his scarred feet with the possibility that he was a foundling. To accept this demands the suspension of disbelief to a remarkable, but evidently not impossible, degree. (Vellacott [1971], p. 189)

There is no evidence that Polybus "refused enlightenment" to Oedipus about the scars on his ankles. For all we know Polybus and Merope did concoct some story to explain them. Nor did Delphi "suggest something mysterious" in Oedipus' relationship with his parents. Rather the oracle was quite specific in predicting what would happen. That it did

---

30. *Ibid.*, p. 191.

not answer the question he asked it left a mystery, but in no way reinforced it.

The major inference the text allows us to draw is that whatever damage and scarring Oedipus suffered, it in no way interfered with his fighting skills. As anyone with a background in martial arts will attest, the lone man who is able — in one encounter, seemingly without injury to himself — to slay a king and four retainers does not suffer from problems with, much less a "terrible reproach" to his ankles or feet. Indeed, the first lesson in self-defense is to run away if possible — preferably having stamped hard on the aggressor's foot so that you cannot be pursued. To say that Oedipus' feet were "malformed" is a gross exaggeration. There is no indication in the text that the adult Oedipus even limped or walked oddly. When one bears in mind what the dialogue implies about Oedipus' fighting prowess, what martial artists all know, and then adds to it the extra bit of information that Sophocles and his intended audience were no strangers themselves to war, combat, and battle, the conclusion is unavoidable that the scars remaining on King Oedipus' feet must have been small and very minor.

(iii) Teiresias' prophetic ability.

In his interview with Oedipus, Teiresias begins by pointing out one of his own failings: what he calls forgetfulness, but what really amounts to a lack of common sense. There is not much sense in coming to a powerful, proud, and easily angered king's court if one thinks that there is a good chance one will then be forced to accuse him of having committed loathsome deeds and being the cause of everything that has recently gone wrong. Oedipus himself cites two other ways in which Teiresias failed as a prophet: he failed to solve the riddle of the Sphinx, and at the time Oedipus was made king in Laius' place and married Laius' widow, he failed to make known *then* what he, albeit reluctantly, alleges *now*.

Teiresias is not omniscient. He does not know all things. Indeed, as Oedipus' criticisms make clear, he is not able to produce on demand. His gift is limited. He cannot force the gods to reveal what he may wish them to reveal. But when the prophetic mode is upon him, he has the truth and is in no doubt about it. He not only knows the significant details of Oedipus' hidden past, he knows Oedipus' future.

For Vellacott the interchange between Oedipus and Teiresias can best be made sense of by assuming that Oedipus knows, at the beginning of the play, that he is Laius' murderer and his wife's son. In it Teiresias repeatedly tells Oedipus that he killed Laius and hints strongly that he is the son of Laius and Jocasta. In his last speech, the blind prophet summarizes what he has said "in clear and emphatic detail"[31].

> During the scene that follows, Oedipus admits that the first of these statements, that he killed Laius, is only too probably true; yet neither he nor the Chorus make any comment on the other statement, but continue to talk as if no such thing had been said. Why? (Vellacott [1971], p. 114)

We fail to find in this scene any indication that Oedipus even considers it possible that he murdered Laius. Neither Oedipus nor the chorus seems to distinguish between (a) an ability to produce prophecy on demand, which Teiresias does not have, and (b) an ability to prophesy the truth when one prophesies, which Teiresias does possess. By reminding those on stage that Teiresias was unable to protect Thebes when it counted, by focusing on an example, the Sphinx's riddle, in which Teiresias was shown to lack (a), Oedipus casts doubt in his own mind and the minds of his audience upon Teiresias' overall abilities as a seer, including (b). Oedipus also casts doubt upon Teiresias' worthiness to be listened to at all, when at the beginning of their interchange he has to *force* him to open up by impugning his motives and making him angry. Finally, it is an exaggeration to say, in such circumstances, that there is a *clear* implication that Oedipus is not the son of Polybus and Merope and that Teiresias' accusations are summarized *clearly* in his final speech. Such clarity is relative to one's audience. To Greek as well as to modern audiences that know the story, these implications and accusations may be clear. But to Oedipus, who is easily distracted and not too smart in the first place and who has also decided not to pay attention to a source he deems both epistemically and morally unreliable, these things are not clear. The chorus, as well, does not know what to make of Teiresias' angry words. Teiresias' last speech is

---

31. [1971], p. 114.

definitely not clear to his audience; it is full of riddles — and, despite his reputation, Oedipus is no good at riddles. Indeed, Teiresias takes aim at precisely this weakness, when he challenges Oedipus to solve the riddles he poses in this last speech.

Oedipus' reaction in line 437 of Vellacott's translation [1971] we take as showing that Oedipus has simply not been attending to Teiresias:

What? What parents? Come back here. Who was my father, then?

Oedipus has tuned out and wants nothing more than to get rid of this pesty prophet, but when Teiresias catches his ear by talking about his "parents", Oedipus asks sarcastically:

What? What parents? Come back here. Who was my father, then *(know-it-all)*?

trying to trip him up, doubting that Teiresias knows anything at all about Polybus and Merope.

Vellacott, however, reads an entirely different meaning into this passage:

In 437 Oedipus, as if caught off his guard, reveals that the certainty about his parentage which he has hitherto implied, and which he is still heavily asserting in 827, and with which orthodox comment credits him, is not certainty at all. (Vellacott [1971], p. 161)

. . . when Teiresias, already on his way out, alludes to "your parents", Oedipus calls him back and asks (437), "What man was my father?" This line alone would make it clear that in this First Episode Sophocles already thinks of Oedipus as the man who remembers the day when Polybus of Corinth lied to him for the last time, and he resolved to go to Apollo for the truth. This line is our first hint of what the Second Episode will make explicit, that Oedipus, when in a rage he pulled Laius from the carriage and killed him, was not securely certain that his father was safe at home in Corinth; to kill this grey-haired stranger was to take a risk which no pious man in those circumstances would have taken, and which, if what he says in 796-7 is honest, he had surely sworn on leaving Delphi never to take. (Vellacott [1971], p. 169)

Again, after the "What man was my father", we should like to insert "if you know so much". Also, if Oedipus really thought that Polybus was lying, why did he exile himself from Corinth after hearing the prophecy? That Oedipus had doubts about his parentage, we agree. That he believed that Polybus was lying, we do not.

Vellacott goes on to argue that the Elders, at least, should be paying heed to Teiresias' words ([1971], pp. 165-66). They all know, quite independently, that Oedipus appeared soon after Laius was killed, that Jocasta's age permits her being Oedipus' mother, and that there is some uncertainty about Oedipus' parentage.

Yet the foundation of Oedipus' case for not heeding Teiresias is factual and also known to the Elders: (a) for some reason, unknown to his audience at the beginning, Teiresias is loath to do what is needed to rid Thebes of the plague by solving the mystery of Laius' murder, (b) Teiresias gets very angry at Oedipus when Oedipus questions his motivation for holding back, (c) when in anger Teiresias does say his piece, he accuses the king himself of the murder, and (d) Teiresias has a history of failure at times when his talent is really needed. Of course, although it, too, "could be true," Oedipus' accusation that Teiresias had complicity in Laius' murder is completely baseless — as baseless, it might seem to the Elders, as Teiresias' own accusation. We can expect Oedipus to go half-crazy when he feels his reputation is being threatened because that is just the kind of person Oedipus is. Line 437 is not an admission of uncertainty about his parents, although Oedipus — if he were more intelligent and less prone to public posturing, anger, and letting his attention wander — might well be, indeed ought to be, more uncertain than he is about the identity of his parents. What motivates his behavior in the Teiresias scene is his desire to play to his public and his extreme defensiveness.

II

Oedipus at Colonus: Part 1

Chronology of Events

The events revealed in the dialogue of *Oedipus at Colonus* seem to necessitate additions and even amendments to the Chronology of Events of *Oedipus Rex*. For example, when Oedipus travelled from Corinth to consult the oracle in Delphi because of the uncertainty about his parentage, the oracle did not settle this question for him, but it did make many other pronouncements. Among these, were there prophecies describing the circumstances of his death?

At the end of *Oedipus Rex* the newly blinded Oedipus says to Creon:

> For me — never let this city of my fathers be thought right to have me as an inhabitant while I live, but allow me to live in the mountains, where the mountain called Cithaeron, this mountain of mine, is situated, which my mother and father, while they lived, set to be my appointed tomb, so that my death may be caused by them who sought to destroy me. Yet this much I know, that neither sickness nor anything else could destroy me. For I would not have been saved from death, if not for some strange fate.
>
> (OT 1449-57)

In this passage Oedipus begs to be left to die from exposure on Mt. Cithaeron, the same fate his parents had planned for him as an infant. He does not sound like a man who knows what is in store for him, the fate described at the end of *Oedipus at Colonus*. Colonus is very near Athens; indeed, it can be located on modern street maps of the city. Mt. Cithaeron, on the other hand, is quite a distance northwest from Athens, closer to Thebes than it is to Athens.

Moreover, in the above passage Oedipus infers that his death will be miraculous from the fact that the gods miraculously allowed him survive as an infant. This way of arriving at what turns out to be an accurate description of the manner of his death does not display the confidence of a man who has heard the Delphic Oracle make detailed pronouncements on the subject — especially when we consider that the blind Oedipus we see in Thebes knows that with respect to forecasting *his* destiny the Oracle has a comprehensive and thus far perfect record of success.

Yet near the beginning of *Oedipus at Colonus* Oedipus says:

> . . . don't be unfeeling towards Phoebus and me, Phoebus who, when he prophesied those many woes, told me of this as a rest after long years, that when I came to a land which was my goal, where I should find a seat of the dread goddesses and a strangers' shelter, there I should reach the end of my wearisome life, with benefits through my settling there for those who received me, but ruin for those who sent me, who drove me away. And he assured me that signs of these things would come, either earthquake, or thunder, or Zeus' lightning.
>
> (OC 86-95)

Indeed, at the end of the play Oedipus, with no hesitation whatever, gives Theseus specific instructions about what must be done in connection with and after his death. This knowledge may also be attributable to the same session with the oracle in Delphi.

The passages cited are clearly in conflict. If we are to view *Oedipus at Colonus* as present and continuing the story begun in *Oedipus Rex*, the chronology of *Oedipus Rex* must be revised, or some very fancy explaining undertaken to smooth this wrinkle away.

Other points of tension between the two plays have to do with expectations raised in *Oedipus Rex* that are entirely overlooked in

Oedipus at Colonus. At the end of *Oedipus Rex*, Oedipus pleads with Creon to cast him out and abandon him to die helplessly in the wilderness. Creon, however, responds:

> I would have done this, be assured, if I did not wish first to learn from the god what should be done.
> (OT 1438-39)

and

> *Oed.*   Do you know, then, on what conditions I shall go?
> *Cre.*   You will speak, and then, on hearing you, I shall know.
> *Oed.*   See that you send me to live away from this land.
> *Cre.*   You ask of me a gift that is the god's to give.
> (OT 1517-18)

In *Oedipus at Colonus* there is no indication of whether Creon pursued his plan to consult the oracle about Oedipus, and if he did, what answer he received. Oedipus bitterly says to Creon:

> Back then, when I was sick with the woes of my own making, when I longed to be exiled from the land, you were not willing to bestow the favour I wished, but when I had had my fill of anger, and living in the house was sweet, then you sought to remove me and cast me out . . .
> (OC 765-70)

When Ismene arrives, Oedipus complains about his sons:

> They, when I, their father, was being disgracefully thrust out from my country, did not stop me or defend me, but I was sent forth by them, driven from house and home, and proclaimed an exile. Will you say that I wanted exile then and that the city reasonably granted me this gift? No![32] For, that very first day, when my anger was boiling, and sweetest for me was death and death by stoning, no one emerged to help me in this desire. But, in time, when all my grief had subsided, and I began to

---

32. Actually Oedipus *did* ask for exile at the end of *Oedipus Rex*. But for him in his condition, newly blinded, being cast out meant death, and he certainly must have realized it.

recognize that my anger had run to excess as too great a punisher of past errors, then at that moment the city sought to drive me by force out of the land after all that time, but they, the sons of the father, though able to help their father, were not willing to act; but, for want of one little word, for their part I went on my wanderings, an exile and a beggar forever.
(OC 427-44)

Oedipus' "in time, when all my grief had subsided" indicates either that his expulsion had nothing to do with any oracular prediction Creon may have solicited at the end of Oedipus' rule as king years before, or that Creon procrastinated for years before he did seek the advice of an oracle, which then confirmed that Oedipus should be exiled. We do not know how the plague that started Oedipus' downfall ran itself out. If it did so swiftly, Creon might have concluded that Oedipus' exile to a blind-man's world of darkness satisfied the original demand that Laius' murderer be banished and not bothered to consult the oracle further. Nonetheless, it is odd that the decision by Thebes to banish him caught Oedipus by surprise: according to *Oedipus at Colonus*, that he would be exiled he heard predicted in Delphi when he originally consulted the oracle. In *Oedipus Rex* he heard Teiresias predict it. Oedipus, one would think, would have spent the years after his downfall waiting for the other shoe to drop. And if Oedipus' sudden expulsion from Thebes was due to some belated prophecy solicited by Creon, why should Oedipus not mention this when he is exchanging accusations with Creon in the second play? After all, Oedipus took an interest in predictions and used Ismene as his "ears" in Thebes to listen for news of them.

At bottom, we simply do not know how the Theban plague ended, or whether Creon consulted the oracle as he said he would at the end of *Oedipus Rex*, or why, all of a sudden, after sufficient time had passed for all Oedipus' grief to subside, a decision was made to send him into exile.

Finally, other important parts of the story of *Oedipus at Colonus* are simply not spelled out as completely as one might wish. How exactly did Oedipus' sons wrong him when he was expelled from Thebes? We at least see Oedipus' daughters in *Oedipus Rex*. We do not see his sons, and his only significant reference to them in the play comes immediately before he asks Creon to care for his daughters:

> But as for my children, Creon, do not take on yourself care for my sons;
> they are men, so that, wherever they are, they can never lack the means
> to live.
>
> (OT 1459-62)

Perhaps the seeds of Polyneices' and Eteocles' future neglect of their
father can be glimpsed taking root here. This brief passage and the lack
of any other reference to his sons does not offer us much evidence of
paternal concern for them on the part of Oedipus.

In any event, it is clear that neither son gave him financial or other
support during his years of mendicant exile afterwards. As the play
opens, we see that Oedipus and Antigone have been living in utter
poverty as wandering beggars, making their slow way along the byroads
of foreign lands. Oedipus does have occasional contact with Ismene in
Thebes. His sons have no excuse for callously ignoring him and not
easing his life in exile. Indeed, at the time of the banishment, they
could have set him up comfortably just outside the frontiers of Thebes
— precisely what Creon proposes to do when he arrives in Athens to
take Oedipus back.

We know, too, that the sons made no protest when Oedipus was
banished. Yet what power did they really possess at the time? Oedipus
says, in his diatribe against Polyneices:

> Villain, you are the one who, when you held the sceptre and the throne
> your brother now holds in Thebes, yourself drove me out, your own
> father, and made me citiless and caused me to wear this dress . . . but I
> must bear this as long as I live, remembering you as my murderer. For
> it was you who made me live in this grief, it was you who thrusted me
> out, and because of you I wander and beg from others my daily
> livelihood.
>
> (OC 1354-57, 1360-64)

What is not clear is the kind of sovereignty Polyneices had before
Eteocles usurped it? Had he already been made king of Thebes? What
powers were then vested in Creon's hands? Oedipus accuses Creon, as
well as his sons, especially Polyneices, of casting him out. We do
know, from *Antigone*, that Creon became king only after Polyneices
and Eteocles had both been slain.

However incomplete the answers are to these questions, it is clear that Oedipus' anger at his sons is justified. They gave their father no aid at all during his long years of exile, and they did not even speak up to defend him when he was cast out of his home in Thebes.

These tensions and gaps between *Oedipus at Colonus* and *Oedipus Rex* have mainly to do with what the circumstances were and what actually happened. Further tensions between the two plays arise from interpretation. For instance, in *Oedipus at Colonus* Oedipus says again and again that he bears no guilt for the events that stain his life, the death of his father and his incestuous marriage with his mother. Yet if the interpretation of *Oedipus Rex* given in Part I is reasonable, Oedipus is wrong about this; he is not a completely innocent victim. He does bear the guilt. Issues like these, which arise from interpretation, will be dealt with in following sections.

Let us continue the Theban chronology, then, starting with the events that occur after the end of *Oedipus Rex*:

28. Oedipus lives on in disgrace in Thebes for many years until he is finally exiled.

29. Oedipus and his eldest daughter, Antigone, then wander as impoverished beggars for years in alien lands.

30. The Delphic Oracle informs Theban petitioners that the safety of Thebes depends upon its taking care of Oedipus, burying him nearby, and honoring his grave in death.

31. As the play opens, Oedipus and Antigone come to a grove near the village of Colonus on the outskirts of Athens. They enter and weary Oedipus sits down to rest. They are told by a passer-by that the grove is sacred to the Furies, that they have trespassed on sacred ground, and that the land they are in is ruled by the king of Athens. Oedipus realizes that he has reached the place where the oracle foretold he would die. He pleads with the man to ask the Athenian king to grant him an interview. The man goes off instead to consult with other local people.

32. Oedipus then prays to the Furies and in doing so reveals the oracle's prophecy concerning his death: that it would happen in a foreign country in a place sacred to the Furies, that those

who give him shelter would be rewarded for it, and that those who cast him out would be cursed.

33. The villagers of Colonus arrive and search for Oedipus and Antigone. The two retreat further into the sacred grove, which the locals fear to enter. Oedipus reveals himself. The locals ask Oedipus and Antigone to come out of the grove so they can be interviewed. They promise not to do them harm. Oedipus and Antigone emerge from the grove and are interrogated by the people of Colonus. Oedipus' identity is soon discovered, and the local people want to cast him out of their country. But Antigone and Oedipus remind them of the promise they have given and of Athens' reputation for offering sanctuary to all who seek it. The villagers decide to let their king, Theseus, settle the matter.

34. Oedipus' other daughter, Ismene, arrives from Thebes bringing news. Oedipus' younger son, Eteocles, has seized power and exiled his elder brother, Polyneices. Polyneices has fled to Argos, where he is raising an army to invade Thebes and oust his brother. Ismene also reports a recent prophecy of the Delphic Oracle which says that Thebes' welfare depends upon its giving shelter to Oedipus, burying him properly when he dies, and honoring his grave. She tells Oedipus that Creon will arrive shortly, planning to take him, willing or not, back to the Theban border and install him just outside it. As a parricide Oedipus is barred from entering Thebes itself.

35. Oedipus pleads with the local people to protect him and promises that if they do, they will reap good fortune. The villagers advise him to make expiation to the Furies for having trespassed into their sacred grove. They explain in detail how this must be done. Ismene offers to perform the ritual on Oedipus' behalf and goes off. The locals then press Oedipus to recount his history. He reluctantly does so, emphasizing that he married his mother completely unknowingly and killed his father in ignorance in self-defense. He proclaims his utter innocence.

36. King Theseus arrives and asks Oedipus what he desires. Oedipus explains that he wants to be buried in Colonus and to have himself and his corpse protected from those who, because

of the recent prophecy of the Delphic Oracle, wish to remove him. Oedipus asks Theseus to promise to protect him. The local people add that Oedipus has spoken of additional blessings they will receive if protection is extended to him. Theseus gives his word and charges the villagers with protecting Oedipus. He exits with his retainers.

37.   Creon arrives with a squad of soldiers. He reassures the local people that he comes as a representative of the city of Thebes to persuade Oedipus to come home to his house in Thebes. Oedipus accuses Creon of lying and wanting only to keep him on the border as a shield against Athens.   Oedipus curses Thebes and says that he and Antigone choose to stay in Colonus. Creon reveals that his men have already taken Ismene prisoner. He then orders his men to seize Antigone and take her back to Thebes.   The soldiers leave with Antigone and Creon himself tries to force Oedipus to go with him. The local people stop Creon, and Theseus arrives.

38.   On hearing what Creon has done, Theseus orders that he not be allowed to leave until Oedipus' daughters are safely returned. He sends his soldiers to stop Creon's men before they reach the border and to retrieve the two girls. Theseus lectures Creon on respecting the laws of both gods and men. Creon argues that Oedipus is so despicable that no one should give him sanctuary and then threatens Theseus with retaliation. Oedipus once again claims complete innocence in the deeds which have made him notorious. He calls upon the Furies to punish Creon. Theseus and his men leave, taking Creon along.

39.   A short time passes, and Theseus returns with Antigone and Ismene, having rescued them from Creon's soldiers. Theseus reports that a relative of Oedipus from Argos has taken sanctuary at Poseidon's altar nearby and is praying that he be allowed to speak with Oedipus. Theseus asks Oedipus to meet him. Oedipus realizes that the man is his son, Polyneices, and asks Theseus not to sanction the meeting. Theseus points out that the sanctuary given Polyneices involves religious custom and urges Oedipus to allow Polyneices to have his say. Antigone also begs Oedipus to meet his son. Oedipus relents.

Theseus departs, leaving some of his soldiers to protect Oedipus.

40. Polyneices arrives and begins by apologizing for his treatment of Oedipus. Oedipus remains stonily silent. Antigone urges Polyneices to keep on talking in the hope that something he will say will move Oedipus to respond. Polyneices then tells his story. Eteocles seized power and forced him into exile. Polyneices journeyed to Argos, married there, and with the aid of six allies from Argos and their armed supporters plans to conquer Thebes and put himself back on the throne. Because of the oracle, he has come to Athens on behalf of his allies and himself to beg Oedipus for his support. With Oedipus' support he is sure he will win and says he will reinstate Oedipus in comfort. Oedipus then accuses Polyneices of being responsible for his present poverty, dependence, and exile, and even calls him his murderer. He prophesies that Polyneices' armies will not take Thebes and that he and his brother will kill each other on the battlefield. He curses both Polyneices and Eteocles. Polyneices, although he believes his cause is lost, vows that he will keep the news of Oedipus' response from his allies and that he will see his plan of attacking Thebes through to the end. Antigone pleads with him to abandon the attack. Polyneices will not relent and asks Antigone to give him a proper burial, should he not survive. Polyneices leaves.

41. It begins to thunder and lightning, and Oedipus, realizing that the time of his death is at hand, begs that a messenger be sent to Theseus asking him to return. Oedipus anxiously awaits Theseus' arrival. Theseus finally comes, and Oedipus explains to him what he must do to gain good fortune for Athens and protection from Thebes if it should attack. He must keep secret the site of Oedipus' interment and pass on the secret to his successor only upon his own death. Oedipus then blesses Theseus and the Athenian people and leads Theseus, his attendants, and his daughters off into the sacred grove.

42. A messenger arrives and tells the local people of Oedipus' death: Oedipus led the group to a great bottomless crack in the earth. There his daughters brought water so he could wash and purify himself. Afterward, amid rumblings from the earth, he

calmed his daughters and said his goodbyes. A low voice from the earth was heard summoning Oedipus. Oedipus asked Theseus to promise to look after his daughters. Then he asked all but Theseus to leave. After a few moments those departing looked back; only Theseus remained with his hand shielding his eyes. Oedipus had mysteriously vanished without a sound. Finally Theseus said a few short prayers and that was all.

43.   Antigone and Ismene emerge from the grove. They mourn Oedipus' death. Theseus arrives, and Antigone requests that she and Ismene be allowed to view his grave. Theseus explains that it was Oedipus' wish that no one be allowed to go where he died. Antigone then asks that Theseus arrange safe passage for her and Ismene back to Thebes, where she hopes to stop the impending battle. Theseus agrees. They leave, and the play ends.

Introductory Remarks

What kind of play is *Oedipus at Colonus*?

Definitely not an Aristotelian tragedy. No major character undergoes a change of fortune for the worse during the course of the play. The essential element of suffering is conspicuously absent in anyone who might qualify as a "hero".

Oedipus himself is better off at the end of the play than he was at the beginning. When the play opens Oedipus is a beggar wandering in exile in foreign lands, homeless, impoverished, often hungry, and entirely at the mercy of strangers. Antigone puts their plight very well, as she attempts to persuade the local people, who have learned Oedipus' identity, not to cast them out.

> . . . on you, as on a god, we depend in our misfortune . . .
> (OC 247-48)

In the closing scenes of the play, however, Oedipus' suffering ends, and he goes to his death without fear. He is now empowered. Although blind, he unhesitatingly leads his daughters, Theseus, and Theseus' retainers deeper into the sacred grove of the Furies toward the place he knows he will die. He knows the circumstances of his death will benefit those who give him sanctuary, and this knowledge empowers Oedipus, who chooses to bestow his gift of good fortune upon Athens and to withhold it from Polyneices and Argos, and from Creon, Eteocles, and Thebes.

With the improvement in Oedipus' fortunes, Theseus' fortunes also improve. So Theseus, too, does not qualify as a tragic hero.

Although she comes to a tragic end in the play that bears her name, in *Oedipus at Colonus* Antigone's fortunes do not decline, and in one sense they arguably improve. For years she has borne the burden of caring for an aging, exiled, penniless blind-man. Oedipus has been banished from Thebes because he committed the crime of parricide. His death frees Antigone to return to her home in Thebes and to carry on with her own life.

Finally, while Oedipus' curses lead us to believe that both Polyneices' and Creon's fortunes will go downhill, this does not happen yet. It is not part of the plot of *Oedipus at Colonus*.

The question of the kind of play *Oedipus at Colonus* is must be explored. But before taking it up, there are two other important features of the play that beg to be addressed. Although *Oedipus at Colonus* does not merely serve to enhance our understanding of the two Theban plays that bracket it, it was written a long time after they were, and it definitely can be read as shedding light upon the events that occur in them.

Oedipus at Colonus satisfies our curiosity about what happens to Oedipus after the terrible denouement of *Oedipus Rex*, and it serves as a guide to what is and is not correct and possible in matters of death and burial to prepare us for *Antigone*, where custom and ritual are turned upside down, the living are buried, and the dead kept unburied. So before discussing *Oedipus at Colonus* as it is in itself, its informative relationships to both *Oedipus Rex* and *Antigone* will first be educed. And to prepare the way for the latter, *Antigone* itself must first be discussed. So the order of presentation will be (1) the interrelationships between *Oedipus at Colonus* and *Oedipus Rex*, (2) the narrow interpretation of *Antigone*, (3) interrelationships between *Oedipus at Colonus* and *Antigone*, and finally (4) the narrow interpretation of *Oedipus at Colonus*.

What Happens to Oedipus

Oedipus is neither an outstandingly honorable man like Theseus, nor even a very nice one. Yet he certainly does qualify as complex and interesting. While its ending is firm and compelling, *Oedipus Rex* leaves us curious about Oedipus' future. What will happen to him? Will he die? Will he be exiled? If he survives, will time and reflection on the disasters he has suffered bring about changes in his character and personality? *Oedipus at Colonus* permits us to follow Oedipus beyond the final scenes of *Oedipus Rex* and to satisfy ourselves about questions like these.

King Oedipus is, not to mince words, a macho posturer whose vanity and ignorance at times leads him to take things to foolish extremes. Now, by the beginning of *Oedipus at Colonus*, Oedipus is blind, exiled, penniless, weak, and helpless:

Oed. Shall I sit?
Cho. Yes, move sideways and sit, crouching low on the edge of the rock!
Ant. Father, this task is mine. Join step to quiet step,
Oed. Ah me! Ah me!
Ant. Leaning your old body upon my loving arm!
Oed. Alas for my malignant doom!
(OC 195-202)

Again:

> But do not leave me alone! For my body would not be strong enough to
> move in isolation or without a guide.
>
> (OC 500-02)

Oedipus is in no position to take public poses and lay down the law,
though his old tendency to take charge peeks out occasionally as he
fusses bossily at his daughters:

> *Oed.* Sit me down, then, and take care of the blind man.
> *Ant.* After so long a time, I do not need to learn this.
>
> (OC 21-22)

> *Oed.* And tell me what occurred as briefly as possible, for a little speech
> is enough for young women.
> *Ant.* This is the man who saved us. You should hear from him, father,
> whose deed it is; thus my part will be brief!
>
> (OC 1115-18)

But he does not seem to rise with the old, characteristic temper, when
Antigone, probably used to his tiny pretensions, pays him back measure
for measure. And even though Creon says:

> For in time, I know, you will come to know this, that you do yourself no
> good now, nor did you in the past, when against your friends you
> indulged your anger, which ever injures you.
>
> (OC 852-55)

we see no evidence that the hair-trigger temper survives.

Oedipus has good reason to be angry with his sons and Creon. But
his anger with them is not displayed in sudden berserk rages. And he
never gets angry with the local people of Colonus, even when they
press him against his wishes to recount his history, or with Theseus,
when Theseus presses him to meet Polyneices, whom he now loathes.
When the local people keep pestering him to recount his story, or when
Theseus pressures him to meet Polyneices, a younger Oedipus might
have suspected that some plot was being hatched against him. The
mature Oedipus does not.

There is only one attack he meets with any suggestion of the old
defensiveness, and unlike the younger Oedipus he allows himself to be

drawn into discussion of it only very reluctantly — his guilt in killing his father and marrying his mother.

Early in *Oedipus at Colonus*, Antigone, who has doubtless heard everything Oedipus has to say a thousand times, characterizes his offenses as having been "committed in ignorance". This characterization Oedipus himself insists upon repeatedly in the play, as failed men will, who over many years get clear about a story — if not the real truth — about themselves.

> And yet how am I evil in nature, I who had been wronged and was retaliating, so that if I was acting with knowledge, not even then would I prove to be evil? But, in fact, knowing nothing, I went where I went . . .
> (OC 270-73)

> I have endured most terrible woes, strangers, endured them (i.e., the blinding) of my own will, as god is my witness; but none of these actions (i.e., the parricide and incest) was my own choice.
> (OC 522-23)

> By an evil marital bed, the city bound me, all unknowing, to the ruin brought about by my marriage.
> (OT 525-26)

> I received a gift, which I, wretched-hearted, ought never have won for having given aid.
> (OC 539-41)

> Caught in the toils of destiny, I murdered and I killed, but in law I am pure: I have come to this state in ignorance.
> (OC 547-48)

> (The killings and the marriage and my misfortunes were things) which I endured to my sorrow by no choice of my own; for the gods wanted it this way, perhaps because they were angry with my family from long ago. For, so far as I myself am concerned, you could not find any crime to reproach me with, in retribution for which I proceeded to commit crimes against myself and my kin. Tell me this: if, by oracles, some ordained doom was coming on my father, that he should die at his children's hand, how could you justly reproach me with this, who had not been begotten by a father or conceived by a mother, but was then unborn? And, if

when I was born in misery, as I was, I fought with my father and killed
him, knowing nothing of what I was doing nor to whom I was doing it,
how can you reasonably fault this deed which I did not intend? And my
mother . . . She was my mother, yes, my mother — alas, my woes! —
I didn't know it, she didn't know it . . . But not of my free will (i.e., innocently) did I marry her, and not of my free will (i.e., willingly) do I
speak now. But I shall not be called an evil man, neither in this marriage
nor in my father's murder which you ever heap on me with bitter
reproaches. Answer me one thing which I ask you: if someone stood by
you and tried to kill you, you "the just man", right here and now, would
you ask if the murderer was your father, or would you immediately
defend yourself?

(OC 963-78, 982-83, 986-94)

Although Oedipus claims ignorance and innocence again and again,
against the background of *Oedipus Rex* his claims are only partly
correct. True, he *was* ignorant of the fact, he did not *know*, that the
old man who forced him off the road and hit him with a stick was his
father. True, he *was* ignorant of the fact, he did not *know*, that the
Theban widow he was marrying was his mother. But in *Oedipus at
Colonus* he neglects to mention that he had unsettled doubts about who
his parents were and that he did receive the Delphic Oracle's prophecy
of dire misfortunes to come between him and whoever his parents really
were. And his memory has entirely transformed his encounter with
Laius from a macho response to insult into an act of self-defense.

Although it is not clear in *Oedipus at Colonus*, Oedipus certainly had
sufficient time to reflect upon what the oracle said and did not say.
Despite two passages in *Oedipus at Colonus* that imply the contrary,
there was no sign that Laius intended to turn back to attack him anew,
or that the stick the old man wielded as his carriage rolled by could in
any sense be thought a lethal weapon. Oedipus' berserk response was
not made in self-defense — in defense, that is, of his life. It was made
in defense of his macho pride.

Oedipus was not compelled to marry Jocasta. Had he not been so
eager to obtain the honors Thebes was offering him for his victory over
the Sphinx, he might have mentioned to his future wife his uncertainty
about his parentage — even though doing so might have jeopardized his

accession to the throne of Thebes.[33]   There is also no hint of this in *Oedipus at Colonus*.

Oedipus, while he undoubtedly believes his protestations of innocence, has let wishful thinking and the many intervening years gild his memory.   This is a conclusion we are entitled to draw when we read *Oedipus at Colonus* against the background of *Oedipus Rex*.   If history had been different and *Oedipus Rex* had not survived, our reading of *Oedipus at Colonus* would be very different.

Public recognition and reputation were paramount for King Oedipus. Do they remain so?

Not to the same degree.

> . . . that very first day, when my anger was boiling, and sweetest to me was death and death by stoning, no one emerged to help me in this desire. But, in time, when all my grief had subsided, and I began to recognize that my anger had run to excess as too great a punisher of past events . . .
>
> (OC 433-39)

Oedipus is a man who through years of suffering and dependency has learned to live with ignominy.   Despite his insistence on his ignorance and innocence, this does represent a mellowing of his character.

While his present situation does not permit him to glory in his power, Oedipus does what its limitations allow him — to curse and bless.   His whole endeavor to persuade the Athenians to protect him and permit him to die in the sacred grove, he means to provide a blessing upon Athens and a curse upon Creon, his sons, and Thebes.

To Creon he says:

---

33. The behavior of Oedipus in this matter is masterfully mirrored in *Oedipus at Colonus* by the behavior of his son, Polyneices, who, in unrestrained pursuit of success and power, vows to keep his doubts secret from his allies and by so doing ensures the destruction of all involved. Indeed, even if custom had dictated that bride and groom not meet prior to their wedding, Oedipus might at least have mentioned this uncertainty to his future wife's brother, Creon.

That will not be yours; what you will have is this: my spirit of revenge upon the country, living there forever.
(OC 787-88)

Therefore to you and to your family may the Sun (Helios), he among the gods who sees all things, grant you a life to live out in an old age such as he has given me.
(OC 868-70)

To Polyneices:

And you, go, loathed by me and disowned, most evil of the evil, taking with you these curses which I call down on you, never to master your native land by force nor to return ever to Argos that lies in a hollow, but by a kindred hand to die and to kill him by whom you were driven out. Such are my curses; and I call upon the dread, paternal darkness of Tartarus, to take you far away from home . . .
(OC 1383-90)

And finally to Theseus:

Bless you, Theseus, for your nobility, and for your just care in our behalf!
(OC 1042-43)

Dearest of friends! I pray that you, and this land, and your followers may be blessed, and in your prosperity remember me when I am dead, for your lasting good fortune![34]
(OC 1552-55)

The younger Oedipus had misplaced pride in a talent for investigation he erroneously thought he had. The blind, older Oedipus, although he still fails to see himself clearly, has definitely gained wisdom. At the end of the play Theseus rightly remarks

---

34. It is interesting that Sophocles adds a further reference to *Oedipus Rex* when at the end of *Oedipus at Colonus* Oedipus commends the care of his daughters to his friend, Theseus, as once he commended it to Creon, who, after the close of *Oedipus Rex*, proved a poor guardian and no friend to Oedipus and his daughters.

You convince me; for I see you prophesy many things and no false utterances. Tell me what I must do!
(OC 1516-17)

Despite rare lapses,

> . . . stay me and place me in a seat, so that we may learn where we are; for as strangers we need to learn from the local people, and to do as they direct.
>
> (OC 11-13)

the greatest change we see in Oedipus is his transformation from a man who seeks the lights of center stage into one for whom privacy and discretion have come to be second nature.

> *Oed.* Child, has the stranger left us?
> *Ant.* He has gone, so that you can say what you will, father, in quietness, since I alone am nearby.
> (OC 81-83)

> *Ant.* Quiet! Some elderly men are coming here, to see where you are seated.
> *Oed.* I will be quiet, and you hide me away from the road in the grove, until I learn what these men will say. For in that knowledge there is security in what we do.
> (OC 111-16)

Oedipus is questioned tenaciously and persistently by the local people, as Teiresias and the Shepherd were once questioned by him, and he now proves as reluctant to answer publicly as they were.

> *Cho.* It is dreadful, stranger, to awaken the old grief that has long been laid to rest; and yet I desire to ask about . . .
> *Oed.* What now?
> *Cho.* The grievous suffering, found irremediable, in which you were implicated.
> *Oed.* Do not, I beg you by the hospitality you grant me, expose by your shameless questioning the things I suffered!
> *Cho.* The tale is widespread and such that it never ceases, and, stranger, I wish to hear it rightly told.
> *Oed.* Alas, alas!

Cho. Consent, I beg you!
Oed. Ah, ah!
Cho. Give me my wish, for I grant yours in all you wish.
(OC 510-20)

Oedipus is reluctant even to meet Polyneices, much less to talk to him. Theseus has to make it clear to Oedipus that not to do so will be a failure to honor religious tradition before Oedipus will bend and agree to a meeting. And when Polyneices appears, Oedipus at first refuses to talk to him or to acknowledge his presence.

The most remarkable symbol the play contains in connection with Oedipus' flight from the limelight is the privacy he requires for his death. The king who insisted on doing everything in public now insists on a private, indeed hidden, death and burial. Of course, Sophocles' plot provides independent motivation for this: Oedipus wishes to bring good fortune to Theseus and Athens. Good fortune will come to the country that shelters him in life and in death. Oedipus worries lest Thebans steal his corpse, take it back to their border, and bury it and honor it there. He thus makes Theseus promise to keep his burial place secret.

Why extract a promise that Theseus will pass the secret on to his successor at his death? First, because it is also essential that Oedipus' grave be honored, and hence someone must know its whereabouts to honor it. Secondly, because it has been predicted that his grave will be the site of a great defeat of his Theban enemies, Theseus' successors must know where it is if they are to incorporate this information for Athens' advantage into a successful military strategy in any future conflict with Thebes.

There is no question of the value *Oedipus at Colonus* has for us simply because it provides a credible and satisfying resolution to issues that linger unresolved at the end of *Oedipus Rex*. There is also no question that, read on its own, without the details of *Oedipus Rex* in the background, *Oedipus at Colonus* is a flatter, less full-blooded and realistic play. Nothing within *Oedipus at Colonus* gives us reason to be suspicious of Oedipus' many assertions that he was entirely innocent in parricide and his incestuous marriage, because he was ignorant of what he was really doing. The Oedipus who in weary old age is wrong about his innocence a long time ago is a far more interesting, vivid, and human figure than the innocent martyr we would be left with in *Oedipus at Colonus*, had *Oedipus Rex* not survived.

Next we turn to an analysis of *Antigone*, the first written, but chronologically last of Sophocles' works about the House of Laius. We shall return several times to *Oedipus at Colonus* to see how it works to help us see through issues raised in *Antigone*.

III

Antigone

Chronology of Events

While many years pass between the end of *Oedipus Rex* and the beginning of *Oedipus at Colonus*, the period that separates *Oedipus at Colonus* from *Antigone* is brief. Also, the events of *Antigone* require neither additions nor amendments to the chronology of *Oedipus at Colonus*. Nor do there seem to be interesting details of fact about this period that are missing. So without further ado we continue the Theban chronology.

44. Antigone and Ismene return to Thebes. Antigone and Haemon, Creon's sole surviving son, are betrothed.

45. Polyneices and his allies from Argos attack Thebes and are defeated. In the battle Polyneices and Eteocles kill each other as Oedipus predicted.

46. Creon assumes the kingship. He decrees that Eteocles be buried with all honors, but that Polyneices, because he is a traitor to Thebes, not be buried or honored in any way, and that any person disobeying this decree be stoned to death.

47. As the play opens, Antigone tells Ismene of Creon's proclamation. Eteocles has already been buried, but Polyneices' corpse lies exposed where he fell. Antigone asks Ismene to help her bury Polyneices. Ismene refuses. Antigone insists that despite Creon's decree it is wrong not to bury Polyneices. She vows to bury her brother and do so publicly. Ismene urges her to act covertly. Antigone and Ismene leave.

48. Creon and the Theban Elders appear. Creon tells them of his proclamation and that he has stationed guards near the corpse to prevent anyone from burying it. He condemns the ruler who does not consult his advisors or puts the interests of friends or relatives before those of the state. He warns them not to intrigue against him.

49. A soldier arrives and reports that some unknown person "buried" Polyneices' body during the night by sprinkling dust on it in a proper manner. The guards, afraid to report their failure to Creon, have chosen by lot the one who should convey this unwelcome news to him. Creon sees a conspiracy and accuses the soldier of taking a bribe. He charges the soldier to find the guilty party and threatens him with torture and death if he fails. Creon leaves. The soldier goes off, planning to flee.

50. The soldier returns with Antigone, saying quite candidly that he had planned to run off, but then had the luck to catch Antigone in the act of burying her brother. The soldier then tells Creon exactly what happened. The guards had brushed the dust off the corpse and were vigilant lest the same thing happen again. Just as the sun was at its apex, a powerful dust-storm arose and made it impossible to see. When the storm abated, Antigone was revealed sprinkling dust over the corpse and mourning. She admitted burying the corpse and did not deny burying it the previous night, and the guards arrested her. Creon dismisses the soldier.

51. Creon asks Antigone whether she was aware of his decree forbidding Polyneices' burial. She acknowledges that she was, but self-righteously insists that the laws of the gods supersede Creon's law. Creon declares that states cannot survive if they allow their laws to be broken and that Antigone must be

punished for her act of defiance. He then accuses Ismene of being Antigone's accomplice and sends for her. Antigone calls Creon a tyrant and says that the Elders agree that she has done what is right, but are afraid to say so. Creon insists that Antigone has opposed the will of the people. Antigone expresses her willingness to die for what she has done.

52. Ismene is brought in, and Creon accuses her of complicity in the crime. She confesses that she is just as guilty as her sister. Antigone denies Ismene's involvement and asks her not to die needlessly. Ismene pleads with Creon not to kill Antigone, his son Haemon's fiance. Creon is firm; Antigone must die. He claims the Elders support his decision by their silence. Antigone and Ismene are taken away by Creon's men.

53. Haemon arrives. Creon lectures him about the duty of a son towards his father. He warns Haemon against being dominated by a woman, especially a confessed lawbreaker. He explains that for the sake of the state a ruler must be firm in seeing that its laws are upheld and in punishing those who break them. Haemon points out to his father that some people do not support his decree and the punishment he has ordained for Antigone. He claims it is his filial duty to listen to what people say and, because of concern for his father's reputation, to warn him when he is about to act unjustly. It is a sign of strength, Haemon claims, to give an ear to others' opinions and to be flexible. Creon refuses to change his decision, and the argument escalates. Creon threatens Haemon and orders that Antigone be brought out to be killed. Haemon will not witness her death and leaves vowing never to see his father again.

54. Creon then orders that both women be punished. At the chorus' urging, he exempts Ismene, but condemns Antigone to be walled up in a cave with food enough to keep her from a quick death. Creon departs.

55. The Elders try to comfort Antigone by telling her that her fame for what she has done will survive her. Antigone will not be comforted. Bitterly she protests having to die because of an unjust law.

56. Creon enters with his guards. He repeats his instruction that Antigone be walled up in a cave with food so that she can

either commit suicide or live on in darkness and solitude. Antigone repeats her claim that she was only doing what the gods have always demanded, and if they have not changed their minds, it is Creon who should be punished. Antigone is led away by Creon's guards to be entombed.

57. Teiresias appears and urges Creon to heed his advice. He says that Creon has offended the gods by not burying Polyneices' body and counsels him to admit his error and bury it at once. Creon responds by accusing Teiresias of having accepted a bribe to get him to reverse his judgment. He swears that Polyneices will never get a burial. Angered by Creon's allegation, Teiresias prophesies that a child of Creon's will die and there will be great mourning in his household because of his refusal to bury Polyneices and his entombment of Antigone. Before he departs, Teiresias adds that the vengeful Furies are now seeking Creon.

58. Teiresias' words frighten everyone, including Creon. The Elders urge Creon to release Antigone and to bury Polyneices properly. Creon resists, but his fear makes him change his mind. He then rushes off with his attendants to put things right.

59. A messenger arrives and tells the Elders that a terrible tragedy has taken place. Two people are dead, one of them Haemon. Creon's wife, Eurydice, appears and asks what has happened. The messenger continues. Creon and his attendants first gave a proper burial to Polyneices and then rushed to the cave where Antigone had been entombed. The soldier who was guarding the cave met them on the way and reported a screaming coming from inside the cave. It was audible as they approached. Haemon had broken into the cave and discovered that Antigone had hung herself. When Creon entered the cave, Haemon tried to kill him and failing, impaled himself upon his sword.

60. Eurydice leaves. The messenger worries about her and follows. Creon arrives and acknowledges that he is responsible for the

deaths of both Antigone and Haemon. The messenger returns with the news that Eurydice has stabbed herself and cursed Creon with her dying breath. Creon describes himself as a man who has killed his wife and son without knowing it. The play ends.

Introductory Remarks

Antigone was the first of Sophocles' Theban plays to be presented to the public. Read in isolation from its companion plays, *Antigone* definitely qualifies as an ideal tragedy in Aristotle's sense, having not one, but two tragic heroes, Antigone and Creon. From what we know from the play taken on its own, neither Antigone nor Creon are pre-eminently virtuous and just, nor downright evil. Both are better than most people, yet each through a great fallibility causes his own ruin. In the wider Theban context, however, Creon is revealed to be evil, and the behavior which on the narrow interpretation constitutes Antigone's "fallibility" now represents the only course of action available to her if she wishes to thwart Creon's machinations.

Consequently, *Antigone's* two protagonists will be discussed in turn. But first there is a puzzle to be resolved. While it may seem that Polyneices' corpse remains exposed until a frightened Creon finally buries it at the very end of the play, the fact is that it gets three proper burials during the course of the play, two times, we are led to believe, by Antigone.

Burials

A very odd feature of *Antigone*, when one stops to think about it[35], is the multiple burial of Polyneices' corpse, which gets buried not once, but three times! Creon knows that Antigone has already buried it when he hurries off to bury it again after Teiresias' prophecy. The soldier who arrests her and brings her in custody to Creon reports that she buried it properly. Indeed, burying it is what Creon sentences her to be punished for. Earlier this same soldier reluctantly confessed that the previous night, while he and his fellow sentries were supposed to be standing guard, some unknown person buried the corpse. Yet if Creon knows the corpse has been properly buried, why does Teiresias' prophecy frighten him into rushing off to bury it again, this time after cremating it?

Perhaps, although the text does not say so, after Antigone buried the corpse and was apprehended by Creon's guards, the guards cleaned the dirt off it as they had earlier. Perhaps this act "unburies" a corpse. Thus Antigone only temporarily succeeds in doing what, in both *Oedipus at Colonus* and *Antigone*, she promises she will do.

On the other hand, suppose that by removing the dust from the corpse, the soldiers do not succeed in undoing its proper burial. Why, then, does Antigone feel the corpse needs to be buried a second time? Why does Creon feel it needs to be buried a third time? If the corpse

---

35. And many commentators have, at least as far back as 1891 when Jebb raised the issue explicitly in [1891], p. 86, note on v. 429.

was properly buried the first time, when the reluctant guard reports to Cleon:

> I am speaking without more ado. Someone has just buried the corpse and gone, after sprinkling thirsty dust on its flesh and performing the rites which were due.
>
> (Ant. 245-47)

and the "someone" is Antigone, why does she come back to do it all over again? Antigone, after all, confesses to performing both burials — at least she does not deny doing so when directly asked. Why does Creon bother to cremate the corpse and bury the ashes? Although when Teiresias makes his appearance, Teiresias is right in thinking that Antigone is improperly buried, he may not know that Polyneices has *already* been properly buried. But Creon does know.

As regards the first two burials, commentators divide, some holding that Antigone performed both[36], others holding that she had nothing to do with the first, but that that burial was the work of the gods or Ismene[37]. We shall come down on the side of those who deny that Antigone performed the first burial. We shall not, however, go further to speculate about who or what was responsible. In our view, the text does not provide enough information to provide a solid answer to this question.

Either a proper burial can be undone and, if so, may have to be repeated, or once properly buried, always properly buried. To bury something is to cover it up. Clearly a corpse *can* be put underground and dug up again. Yet, as with marriage and Christening, burial of the

---

36. See Jebb [1966], Bradshaw [1962], Knox [1964], and Whitehorne [1983].

37. See Rouse [1911], Adams [1931], and McCall [1972]. For further general discussion of denial of burial in ancient Greece, see Rosivach [1983], Parker [1983], and Held [1983].

dead is widely taken to have *ritual* aspects[38]. Moreover, just as the ritual of Christening may in certain circumstances be accomplished without total immersion, by a mere sprinkling of water, so in certain circumstances burial rites may, we wish to suggest, be accomplished without sinking the corpse totally underground, by a mere "sprinkling of thirsty dust". After the appropriate persons (like Antigone) have undertaken and accomplished the ritual burial, the rest of the job, the sweaty, back-breaking task of covering a corpse completely under a permanent blanket of earth without aid of steel digging tools, may have been relegated to servants or slaves.

It is clear from the text that the first and second burials of Polyneices' corpse were ritual ones. Can ritual burials be undone by removing the "sprinkling of thirsty dust"?

Assume that ritual burials can be undone. The further assumption — not supported by textual evidence — that the guards undid the second burial will then help to explain why Creon hurries off to bury Polyneices' corpse a third time after Teiresias frightens him. But having arrived at the corpse in the dust storm, when none of the guards can see her, Antigone should seize the moment, bury her brother properly, and leave before the storm blows itself out. The guards will then be none the wiser, and thinking the body has not been given the rites of burial, but just dusted by the storm, they will not bother to clean the dust off and "unbury" it a second time. By sticking around and wailing loudly after the storm, Antigone behaves in a manner that ensures the failure of the project she is willing to give her life for — the (permanent and proper) burial of her brother's body. Assuming she is the one who performed the burial rites over the corpse the first time, she knows what will happen if the guards discover that she has done so again. She

---

38. That in the context of ancient Greece there was a distinction between performing ritual burial rites and putting a body completely underground is denied by Whitehorne [1983], p. 129.

knows that they will undo any burial they know has been performed[39]. So if her true aim, her primary purpose, is to get her brother buried properly and permanently, and she is not incredibly stupid, she knows she *must* act surreptitiously.

Does she? She does not even plan to do so. She says to Ismene,

> That's how matters stand, and you will soon show whether you are noble, or the cowardly daughter of a noble race.
> (Ant. 37-38)

> I certainly intend to bury my brother, and yours, if you will not, for I will not be found betraying him.
> (Ant. 45-46)

> It will be noble for me to die in doing that. I shall lie with him, a loved one with a loved one, a criminal whose crime was righteous . . .
> (Ant. 72-74)

Antigone is not merely interested in performing Polyneices' burial rites; she wants it to be *known* that she has done so.

> *Ism.* At least reveal this deed to no one! Keep it hidden, and I'll do the same!
> *Ant.* Oh, declare it! I shall hate you much more for your silence, if you do not announce these things to all.
> (Ant. 84-87)

This is reinforced later in the play when Ismene claims part of the credit for defying Creon's edict and Antigone rebukes her,

---

39. Bradshaw remarks "They (the watchmen) sweep off the dust . . . because they know very well that anyone who cares for the dead man enough to bury him cannot observe such desecration unmoved", [1962], p. 207. This may indeed be what motivates the watchmen. But it does not explain what would motivate Antigone to appear a second time to sprinkle dust if she does not know it has been removed and she does know that she will be stopped before she can complete a full burial. And why return to sprinkle more if she does know it has been and *will be* removed?

But justice will not allow you this, since you were not willing to take part, nor did I give you a share.

(Ant. 538-39)

Here is what the guard who arrested her says:

. . . we sat on top of a hill, to windward, taking care that the smell from him should not strike us, every man alertly keeping the man next to him awake with torrents of abuse, in case anyone should neglect the task at hand. This went on for some time until the sun's bright circle had taken its place in the middle of the sky, and the heat began to burn us. And then suddenly a whirlwind raised from the earth a dust storm, a trouble in the sky, and it filled the plain, ruining all the foliage of its woods; and the wide sky was filled with it. We shut our eyes and bore the plague sent by the gods. And when after a long time this had departed, the girl was seen, and she cried out bitterly the sharp cry of a bird, when in its empty nest it sees the bed without its young. So she also, when she saw the corpse bare, cried out in lamentation, and uttered dread curses on those who had carried out the deed. And immediately she brought thirsty dust in her hands, and from a pitcher of wrought bronze held aloft she crowned the corpse with a threefold libation.

(Ant. 411-31)

Antigone arrives at precisely the wrong time to do anything surreptitiously — at high noon. Luck is with her, though. A powerful, blinding duststorm blows up and gives her ample time to bury her brother without the guards or anyone catching on. But she stupidly dawdles, the duststorm ends, and she gets caught.

Yet perhaps she arrived too late, when the dust storm was abating. Then *if* her aim is to get the burial rites done properly and permanently, she must simply bide her time until a more propitious occasion presents itself.

The guard is under the impression that Antigone is outraged to find her earlier burial undone. Can he be right? Can her actions be explained as follows?

She gives Polyneices proper burial rites (given the circumstances) the first time at night, knowing of Creon's edict, but not imagining that he might check on the corpse or post a guard over it, and is outraged to discover the next day that he has and that the first burial has been undone. By luck she just happens to be carrying the right ceremonial bronze pitcher with the right stuff in it for a burial libation and decides on the spot that the best way to proceed to get the body buried with no danger of anyone undoing the burial a second time is by performing the ritual there and then out in the open at high noon[40].

This is ridiculous. Like her father Antigone is a public posturer. She has no false pride, but she is stubborn and full of self-righteousness. Nevertheless, she *does* want her brother buried properly and permanently. Sophocles gives us no reason to think she is dumb enough to behave in a way that ensures the frustration of this goal, however self-destructive she is in her insistence on challenging Creon overtly head-on afterwards. So, since (a) Antigone primarily wants her brother's corpse buried, both ritually and literally, and (b) since she performs the rites openly realizing that she will be caught and his corpse exposed anew, we can conclude that Antigone believes that burial rites properly performed cannot be undone — that those she expects will expose Polyneices' corpse when she is discovered will not succeed in undoing the ritual burial she has given it. Since this is what Antigone believes, we, too, must reject the assumption that burial rites can be undone. The corpse can be dug up and abused. Doing so is bad. But it does not undo whatever rites have been properly performed.

So why, then, if Antigone had buried her brother's corpse surreptitiously at night, does she come equipped to do so again at high noon? If Antigone had performed the burial the night before, there would be no reason for her to return to bury Polyneices the next day at all — even though the guards cleaned off corpse early that morning — since she believes that burial rites cannot be undone. But Antigone did turn up to bury her brother the next day. So she was not the person who performed the surreptitious burial the night before.

Let us assume that Antigone is true to her word. She wants it to be known that she buried her brother. She brings with her the proper equipment to bury her brother's body because she wishes to perform the

---

40. Bradshaw suggests that returning to the burial site to pour additional libations was a common custom, [1962], pp. 208-09. But Antigone also first "sprinkled thirsty dust".

burial rites properly, not because she has *already* done so and wishes for some odd and unknown reason to do so again. But given what has happened and what is assumed in the guards' line of questioning, the self-righteous woman who wants to be credited publicly for defying Creon and burying her brother, has no reason to deny being the first to bury him. As far as she is concerned, if this means she will get a little extra credit, good. After all, Ismene also takes credit for Polyneices' burial, and we know she has had nothing whatever to do with the second burial.

It is not Antigone's style to bury Polyneices surreptitiously at night, and on the assumption that one burial is sufficient, her arrival with the proper equipment at high noon argues against the guards' quick assumption that she was the one who performed the first burial[41]. The first, surreptitious burial at night was, if anything, more in the style of Ismene[42], but Sophocles has not given us enough evidence to enable intelligent speculation as to who really did it. We are in a position to say, however, that it is extremely unlikely Antigone did.

Why has Sophocles even bothered to insert the first burial into the play at all — if it must ever remain a mystery who performed it? One can only speculate. Its function in the play might simply be to set limits concerning burial rites — to inform audiences how little needs be done in the way of interment to give a corpse a proper burial, just "sprinkling thirsty dust on its flesh and performing the rites which were due".

There remains the question of why Creon feels it necessary to bury the body a third time, knowing that it has already been buried twice. There are at least two reasons: Because he was the one who caused Polyneices' body to be exposed and dishonored in the first place, he himself has to make atonement for it; and because the corpse received

---

41. The difference in styles of the burials — the first by night, silent and surreptitious, the second at high noon, with loud keening and abandon — has been remarked by McCall [1972], p. 106.

42. That Ismene performed the first burial was suggested by Rouse [1911], pp. 40-42.

only abbreviated, ritual burial, far less than complete interment, it is still not literally under the ground and has come to be in a such a state that it now requires special treatment — if only for reasons of public hygiene. The messenger reports to Eurydice,

> I attended your husband as his guide to the furthest part of the plain, where Polyneices' body still lay unpitied and it had been torn apart by dogs. We prayed the goddess of the roads (i.e., Hekate) and Pluto to restrain their anger and to be merciful; we washed the body with holy washing, and among freshly cut branches we burned what was left; and we raised a high burial-mound of his native earth . . .
> (Ant 1196-1204)

To conclude: Antigone was not the person who first buried Polyneices. Despite what the soldier and Antigone say, whoever it was remains a mystery. Creon buries the corpse a third time in an endeavor to atone for what he has done and because the body is now in a state that requires special treatment.

Creon in *Antigone*

1. The Narrow Interpretation

Oedipus is a paradigmatic Aristotelian tragic hero. There are many parallels to *Oedipus Rex* in *Antigone*, and while Antigone definitely shows herself to be her father's daughter, most of these have to do with similarities between the behaviors of Creon and Oedipus.

Creon is now King. The source of Creon's problems has to do with his public persona. Royal decrees are essentially public. Just as Oedipus gets himself into trouble immediately the play opens by publicly undertaking to find and to punish the murderer of Laius, even if the culprit should turn out to be himself, so in *Antigone* Creon starts off with a decree and a promise to punish whoever breaks it, even if that person should turn out to be someone close to him:

> . . . nor would I ever hold as my friend a man who was my country's enemy . . .
>
> (Ant. 187-88)

Creon is even quicker than Oedipus to look for conspiracies against his rule. In his first address as King to the assembled Elders he says:

> *Cho.* What then is this additional order you would give?
> *Cre.* That you not side with those who disobey these commands.
>
> (Ant. 218-19)

Like Oedipus, Creon is intolerant of criticism and defensive in the extreme, to the point of disloyalty to those closest to him. At the merest whiff of disagreement, he attacks:

> *Cho.* Lord, for some while my mind has been advising that this deed
> might perhaps be even the work of the gods.
> *Cre.* Stop before by your words you have filled me full of anger . . .
> (Ant. 278-81)

He responds with immediate accusations of conspiracy. He suggests that there are conspirators among the Elders. He accuses the soldier of taking a bribe to abet a conspiracy. He accuses Ismene of conspiring with her sister. And finally, like Oedipus, he accuses Teiresias of taking bribes in return for making up prophecies. He refuses to listen to the advice of his own son.

At the end, like Oedipus, he claims innocence because of ignorance:

> Please lead me out of sight, a foolish man, who killed you, my son,
> unknowingly, and you too, my wife — wretch that I am!
> (Ant. 1339-41)

Creon, like Oedipus, is pig-headed and arrogant. Although he does not have Oedipus' great pride in his supposed wisdom and perspicacity, Creon, like Oedipus, does fail to distinguish himself by intelligence or cleverness. During the course of the play, Creon makes no less than eight blunders.

His proclamation is, of course, a major one. Right, tradition, and the gods do not demand *equal* honors in burial, but they do demand burial. Creon is, of course, absolutely correct in characterizing Polyneices as a traitor:

> . . . who, on his return from exile, sought to burn from top to bottom his
> ancestral land and the gods of his family, and sought to taste kindred
> blood and to lead other kin into slavery . . .
> (Ant. 199-202)

As far as possible, compatible with giving custom and the gods their due, honors *should* be withheld from Polyneices.[43] But Creon's decree goes much too far.

While he occasionally gives lip service to the wisdom of seeking and taking advice, Creon consistently refuses to hear opinions that conflict with his own until it is too late. He rudely shuts the Elders up, while saying that their silence condones what he has done. He shuts up the soldier. He pays no heed to his son's advice when his son urges him to listen to the advice of others. And at first he even turns a deaf ear to the advice Teiresias has come to give him.

Creon mistakenly attributes unworthy motives to others. At one time or another he accuses the Elders, the soldier, Ismene, and Teiresias of conspiring against him. He accuses his son of being unmanly and led by the nose by his fiance, Antigone.

Although he is right in thinking that Ismene knows about Antigone's plan to bury Polyneices, he is mistaken in charging her with having aided her sister in burying him.

He behaves with arrant stupidity when he singles out the soldier to find the person who first buried Polyneices and threatens him with torture and death if he fails.

Creon is mistaken in the severe punishment he metes out to Antigone and in thinking that if he commands that food be left with her when she is walled up in the cave, he will not be responsible for her death.

He mistakenly defends the authority of the state, when a far more important component, justice, is conspicuously missing from it.

Finally, when Teiresias frightens him into attempting to remedy the situation, and the Elders advise him about what he must do:

---

43. One of the clever features of the construction of *Oedipus at Colonus* is that in it Sophocles shows us that Creon knows precisely the right kind of burial a traitor like Polyneices deserves (a burial somewhere outside Thebes), that Creon has respect for neither custom nor the gods, and, indeed, that he does not qualify as a tragic hero at all.

Go and release the girl from the underground chamber, and with due rites make a tomb for the unburied dead.
(Ant. 1100-01)

Creon goes about things the wrong way around by first burying the dead man and only then going to unbury the live woman!

This last, seemingly incredible blunder is only one of a small number of suggestions in the play that by forbidding Polyneices' burial Creon has been playing a more sinister game. In Sophocles' day the cremation of a body took a lot of time — for wood to be gathered, piled, lit, and for the fire to do its job. Why, indeed, aside from sheer stupidity, should he leave Antigone walled up in her cave while he *first* goes about cremating and then burying her brother, unless he really prefers to give Antigone even more time to suffer, to abandon hope and succumb, or to kill herself before he does get around to exhuming her?

At the beginning of the play Antigone remarks to Ismene,

Such, they say, is the proclamation that the good Creon has made to you and me — to me, I tell you — . . .
(Ant. 31-32)

In one sense, this comment is perfectly innocent. Who else would such a decree be aimed at? The state will bury its heroes, including Eteocles. But Antigone and Ismene are the only blood relatives Polyneices has left, so they are the only persons in Thebes who are even likely to be interested in personally taking a hand and giving a traitor like him a decent burial.

Yet Creon is newly installed on the throne. He claims his kingship as next of kin. Kin he is, but by his dead sister's marriage to Laius and Oedipus, not by bloodline. Later in the play, Teiresias observes,

But concede to the dead, and do not stab a fallen man! What prowess is there in killing again the dead?
(Ant. 1029-30)

Teiresias' question raises an interesting point. It is not good to give a traitor of Polyneices' ilk equal honors to the heroes who died defeating him and saving Thebes. It is best to tuck him away properly, quietly, at a distance, unhonored. But why should Creon carry the matter further than this and mistreat the corpse — unless he foresees that the effect of doing so will come to rest ultimately upon the living? And where else is it going to land, save upon Antigone and Ismene?

If we fix only upon what we learn from *Antigone*, we find just two further clues. Antigone, now condemned, laments,

> You touch on my most painful thought, on the lamented lot of my father and on the entire destiny that is ours, the famous house of Labdacus. Ah, the calamities of a mother's bed! Ah, the wretched mother's incestuous couplings with my father — from what kind of parents was I born, their wretched daughter! To them I go thus, accursed, unwed, to live with them. Ah, my brother, who made an ill-fated marriage, in your death you have destroyed me while I still live.
> (Ant. 857-71)

Before the opening of the play, Antigone and Creon's son, Haemon, were formally betrothed. Creon has had to wait years to accede to the throne. The royal bloodline of Thebes still survives in Antigone and Ismene. Creon may find Haemon's marriage to Antigone objectionable for one of two reasons: First, as Antigone points out, marriages in Laius' line are proven disasters. Is this what he wants for his sole surviving son? Secondly, his son's marriage to Antigone may attenuate his own hold on the throne, which, as his preoccupation with conspiracies perhaps indicates, may not yet be very firm. Creon does his best in his discussion with Haemon to characterize Antigone negatively, not merely as a lawbreaker, but as an enemy and conspirator who uses her sexuality to dominate.

The second hint comes when Creon in his opening speech promises to punish anyone who defies his decree, *even if it should be someone close to him.* Oedipus' promise to root out and exile or kill the murderer of Laius *even if it should turn out to be himself* conveys no possible sense of hidden intrigue, just political rhetoric. But the qualification Creon inserts makes his pronouncement sound suspiciously like he may be attempting to create in advance, with eyes raised piously heavenwards and hands innocently open, an appearance of impartiality for later, when he will bring down the full force of the law upon those parties he has already had in his cross-hairs to target with his decree.

We do not wish to claim that these speculations about Creon's motivation are anything more than what they are, speculations. Indeed, they are destined to remain so even when Sophocles in *Oedipus at Colonus* furnishes us with further solid evidence of Creon's capacity for malevolence and with amplified motive. That Oedipus does not have a talent for detection is, to our minds, established beyond doubt, as is the fact that Antigone does not bury her brother twice. But whether Creon operates from sinister motives in issuing his decree that Polyneices not be buried is by no means so certain. Yet what we read in *Oedipus at Colonus* does, we believe, add significantly to its plausibility.

2. The Theban Context

If we focus upon *Oedipus at Colonus* alone, Oedipus' repeated claims about his innocence and acting in ignorance seem very believable, but in the wider Theban context which includes *Oedipus Rex* it is obvious that they are only half-truths. Similarly, if we focus upon *Antigone* alone, Creon seems to qualify by Aristotelian standards as a tragic hero. But when viewed in the Theban context which includes *Oedipus at Colonus*, this appearance vanishes completely. Creon is no hero at all, but a smooth-talking villain, and Aristotle definitely rules out "the passing of a bad man from good fortune to bad fortune" as providing an appropriate plot for dramatic tragedy.

Although *Oedipus Rex* may contain some indications that Creon is not entirely on the up-and-up, Teiresias there firmly closes the door on the possibility.

Oed. Whose idea was this, Creon's?
Teir. No, Creon is no trouble to you; you are your own!
(OT 378-79)

Real questions about Creon begin to surface during the long period between the end of *Oedipus Rex* and the beginning of *Oedipus at Colonus*. Did or did not Creon consult the oracle about Oedipus, as he said he would at the end of *Oedipus Rex*? Why was Oedipus not banished immediately his parricide and incest became known? Why, if not immediately, was he banished at all? Why the long delay? The end of *Oedipus Rex* makes it clear that Creon held the reins of power before Polyneices and Eteocles came into their majority. Indeed, Ismene reports that the brothers first wanted to leave the governing of Thebes to Creon. How did Creon react when they changed their minds? Did Creon have anything to do with Polyneices and Eteocles' failure to support their father at the time when Oedipus finally was sent into exile? Was it Eteocles' own idea to plot against Polyneices, or did he do so with Creon whispering in his ear? These are questions readers of the Theban trilogy would like answers to — questions that it unfortunately does not proffer much promise of answer.

But *Oedipus at Colonus* does make certain facts concerning Creon perfectly clear. First, Creon is shown to be fully aware of a way in which a traitor's corpse can be disposed of without giving insult to the gods or tradition. Polyneices could be buried in much the same way Creon earlier had planned to bury Oedipus — in a grave that is not on Theban soil, but just beyond its borders. If it is wrong to bury Oedipus within Thebes because he is guilty of regicide and parricide, Polyneices, as a traitor, does not deserve better. While Antigone and Ismene, the two surviving members of his bloodline, will doubtless wish to perform whatever funeral rites the ties of kinship call for, they will be doing so outside the borders of Thebes and will not be seen by Thebans to be honoring a traitor within the homeland he betrayed. We know from *Oedipus at Colonus* that Creon is alert to this option. Why, then, does he not avail himself of it? Why, instead, does he produce a decree he knows will strike directly at Antigone and Ismene? This unanswered question further fuels the suspicion raised in the last section that Creon's actions spring from sinister and not from high-minded but mistaken motives.

The information about Creon's character that is revealed in *Oedipus at Colonus* lends further plausibility to this idea. Creon appears just once, but his villainy is immediately obvious. We already know from Ismene's report, before he even arrives in Colonus, that he comes to take Oedipus, hold him prisoner, and ultimately bury him just outside the Theban frontier, because Oedipus, the oracle says, will provide safety to the state that honors his grave. We soon learn that before Creon even appeared in Colonus he already had his men take Ismene captive, and she is at that very moment being carried off to Thebes.

Creon comes to Athens with armed men to do his bidding if he fails to achieve the results he wants with words.

Against the background of these facts, Creon's rhetoric is clearly misleading, full of lies, and hypocritical. He is hypocritical in playing up Antigone's suffering, poverty, and vulnerability. Oedipus and Antigone have received no help to relieve their suffering, poverty, or vulnerability from Creon or anyone else in their family, save Ismene. He misleads when he claims that all Thebes wants Oedipus back — without mentioning the latest oracle and why. Creon lies when he explains the Thebans' desire that Oedipus return by saying that everyone is at fault for Oedipus' suffering, and the general wish is to atone for it. He lies when he says he wishes to install Oedipus in his father's house. He lies when he says to Theseus that he did not expect the Athenians to give asylum to Oedipus: he arrived in Athens with soldiers, and he took the precaution of kidnapping Ismene *before* he approached Oedipus. Indeed, earlier, when his men were carrying off Antigone and when he was attempting to take away Oedipus, the villagers of Colonus told him to stop because Oedipus and Antigone *had been granted* asylum. He lies when he tells Theseus that his use of force was in response to Oedipus' curses, when the situation was just the reverse — Oedipus cursed him because he had forcefully taken his daughters and was attempting to abduct him.

Creon pays heed only to force. He works singlemindedly for his own ends — whether by rhetoric or naked power — and ignores others'. In kidnapping Ismene and Antigone and in attempting to abduct Oedipus, Creon flouts the laws and customs of Athens. By abducting Oedipus and his daughters from the grove, he flouts the institution of sanctuary that is sacred to the gods. Against what we learn of his character from *Oedipus at Colonus*, it comes as no surprise that in *Antigone* he works singlemindedly to uphold his authority, at the expense of justice.

Finally, we are given in *Oedipus at Colonus* one further reason why Creon might wish to bring Antigone and Ismene down. To Creon in *Antigone*, the newly crowned king of Thebes, Antigone and Ismene are constant reminders of the ignominious failure of his mission to Athens. He not only failed to protect Thebes, in light of the oracle's pronouncement, by bringing Oedipus back, he underwent the humiliation of being forced by Theseus to return Antigone and Ismene whom he had abducted and taken hostage. He had been shown up in front of his soldiers. Doubtless, all Thebes soon heard about the debacle. This, as well as concerns about the consequences of Haemon's marriage to Antigone, might indeed explain why he strikes at her by issuing a decree he knows she will find it impossible to obey. It may also explain his haste to indict Ismene. What remains unexplained is why Creon relents and exempts Ismene from Antigone's punishment. He has thus far had the Elders sufficiently cowed so that none voiced objection to his actions, however outrageous. Perhaps he fears that the inclusion of Ismene would spark more active opposition than the disgruntled mumblings Haemon speaks of.

Antigone in *Antigone*

1. The Narrow Interpretation

Antigone is definitely her father's daughter. In the matter of her brother's burial, at least, she singlemindedly and stubbornly pursues public recognition. She is not willing *just* to give Polyneices a proper funeral. This she could do surreptitiously without Creon or anyone else being the wiser. No, as we have seen earlier, Antigone wants to be *known* as the dutiful sister who defied the king's wicked decree and did what was right and proper at the cost of her life:

> That's how matters stand, and you will soon show whether you are noble, or the cowardly daughter of a noble race.
> (Ant. 37-38)

> I certainly intend to bury my brother, and yours, if you will not; for I will not be found betraying him.
> (Ant. 45-46)

> It will be noble for me to die in doing that. I shall lie with him, a loved one with a loved one, a criminal whose crime was righteous . . .
> (Ant. 72-74)

> *Ism.* At least, reveal this deed to no one! Keep it hidden, and I'll do the same!

> *Ant.* Oh, declare it! I shall hate you much more for your silence, if you
> do not announce these things to all.
> (Ant. 84-87)

But justice will not allow you this, since you were not willing to take
part, nor did I give you a share.
(Ant. 538-39)

> *Ant.* Do you want anything more than to take and kill me?
> *Cre.* I want nothing more. When I have that, I have everything.
> *Ant.* Why then do you delay? In your words there is nothing that
> pleases me, and I pray there never may be! And so my views are
> displeasing to you too. And yet how could I have won more
> glorious fame than by giving burial to my own brother?
> (Ant. 497-504)

Once again, if we narrow our focus to *Antigone* itself, its heroine's
desire not *merely* to do what is right and bury her brother, but to be
known and, indeed, famous for it, qualifies, in Aristotle's sense, as a
great fallibility. By her actions Antigone self-destructively asks for,
insists upon punishment. She acts with such public self-righteousness
that Creon must lose face if he fails to punish her. And once caught,
she never stops proclaiming the rightness of what she has done and the
injustice of what Creon is doing to her.

It has already been noted that *Antigone* contains some indications of
a sinister side to Creon — that his decree is intentionally designed to
provoke Antigone, her sister, and no one else into becoming law-
breakers. The play also contains a suggestion that Antigone's self-
destructive persistence in going public and self-righteously challenging
Creon is not just an unsurprising feature of her character, given she is
her father's daughter, but is part of a deliberate course of action she
adopts in order to cause Creon's downfall.

The Theban Elders are spineless and wishy-washy, completely cowed
by Creon. But Antigone is correct in thinking that they are enough in
awe of the gods and tradition to agree in their hearts that, despite
Creon's decree, by burying her brother she was doing what was proper.
When she makes her last appearance, they say,

And now at this sight I too am carried beyond the laws, and can no longer restrain the streaming tears, when I see Antigone passing to the bridal chamber where all sleep.
(Ant. 801-05)

But the Elders are too timid to come out and state that Antigone's actions are right, and risk implying publicly that Creon's decree is wrong. Creon has warned them in the beginning about intrigue, subversion, and aiding dissidents. Instead, they try to comfort Antigone by telling her how heroic she has been and how famous she will be after death. But Antigone will not allow them to spin comforting or rosy stories and silently put to rest what their consciences know to be true.

Oh, I am mocked! Why, by our fathers' gods, do you insult me not when I am dead, but to my face? O city, O wealthy men of the city! Ah, Dirce's springs and sacred ground of Thebes, city of fine chariots, at least I acquire you as witnesses, in what manner I go, unwept by friends, and by what laws I go to the heaped mound of my strange tomb. Ah me wretched! to dwell neither among the living nor a corpse among corpses, not with the living, not with the dead!
(Ant. 839-52)

Antigone is relentless in proclaiming her innocence. She will not let the Elders forget it. Their timid question,

Do you really intend to kill them both?
(Ant. 770)

has made Creon back down about making Ismene share Antigone's fate. Antigone's speeches seem entirely aimed at stiffening whatever little moral fiber the Elders have, so that they will begin to stand up to Creon.

Why in my misery should I look any more to the gods? What ally should I call upon? When by my pious act I have acquired the repute of impiety. Well, if these things are good in the court of the gods, by my suffering I shall come to know that I have done wrong; but if these men are doing wrong, may they experience no greater woes than they are unjustly working out on me!
(Ant. 922-28)

She persists in addressing and challenging them to her very last speech,

> O city of my father in the land of Thebes, and O ancestral gods, I am
> being led away, my time has come! Behold me, princes of Thebes, the
> only remaining daughter of your kingly house! Behold how I am treated,
> and by what kind of men, for revering the reverence of piety.
>   (Ant. 937-43)

Unfortunately, it is only after Teiresias arrives and delivers his
terrifying prophecies that the Elders finally are willing to venture a
meek

> There is a need for wise counsel, son of Menoiceus!
>   (Ant. 1098)

The suggestion we are putting forward here is that Antigone is
attempting to cause Creon's downfall the only way she can — by
publicly defying his proclamation, by publicly insisting at every opportunity on the rightness of her actions and the injustice of his, and by
being made a martyr by him.

Thus there are two interpretations of what Antigone is doing in the
play. Under the first, Antigone has a great fallibility — she is a self-
righteous fool and unnecessarily brings upon herself her own death.
Under the second, her only weakness is in thinking, if indeed she does,
that her course of action in burying her brother and criticizing and
defying Creon publicly at every turn will be sufficient to bring Creon
down. She is extremely brave — in that when she begins her public
struggle with Creon she cannot foresee whether her actions will indeed
produce this effect. She is definitely not in a position to know that a
Teiresias will appear and push to completion the events she has set in
train.

On the first interpretation, *Antigone* qualifies as an ideal Aristotelian
tragic heroine. On the second, she does not; she has no great fallibility.
She is simply doing her best to make the conditions favor the end she
seeks. Being unable to guarantee the results she wants is no great fallibility. It is the kind of weakness we all suffer from. Wishing to
provide for our children's future and being unable to guarantee we will
live to see them safely into adulthood, we take out life insurance. But

still, however much we would wish to, we cannot guarantee the long-run solvency of the company that carries our policies.

2. The Theban Context

Once we extend our focus beyond the narrow interpretation, it is immediately clear that Creon is really a villain and not a tragic hero at all. What do we learn about Antigone herself when we look beyond *Antigone* to *Oedipus Rex* and *Oedipus at Colonus*?

We discover in *Oedipus at Colonus* that Antigone and Polyneices are very close. Unlike Oedipus, Antigone has completely forgiven Polyneices his failure to provide even a minimum of assistance during the long, impoverished exile she has shared with her blind father. Antigone loves her brother deeply. It is more than familial duty and more than just the promise she made that moves her to give Polyneices a proper burial. She plays a crucial role in persuading the very obdurate Oedipus to meet with him. When Polyneices does arrive and Oedipus will still not acknowledge his presence, she attempts to mediate. She does all she can to persuade Polyneices to call off his projected attack on Thebes. She cajoles, she begs, she cries.

> *Ant.* Ah, wretched me!
> *Pol.* Do not mourn for me!
> *Ant.* And who would not lament for you, brother, who rushes to a death foreseen?
> *Pol.* If it is my fate, I will die.
> *Ant.* No, no! Do what I ask!
> *Pol.* Do not ask what cannot be!
> *Ant.* Then I am truly wretched, if I must lose you.
> (OC 1438-43)

Antigone is also an eye-witness to Creon's attempts, first by words — hypocrisy, lies, half-truths — and then by force, to take and keep captive her father. Indeed, she and her sister are themselves abducted by Creon and saved only by her father's new Athenian protectors. The righting of wrongs — his treatment of her father, her sister, herself, and her dead brother's corpse — provides quite a sufficient motive for a tough lady like Antigone to risk her life in an attempt to defeat Creon.

The further information about Antigone which is found in *Oedipus at Colonus* favors the second interpretation mentioned earlier. Antigone has no great fallibility of excessive self-righteousness and pursuit of public recognition. Her blatant, confrontational behavior in response to Creon's attack is really the only hope she has of defeating Creon. And, indeed, while the tactic does not in itself succeed, it does lay the groundwork for his defeat. If we view *Antigone* from a wider context which includes the play whose chronology precedes it and accept this interpretation, *Antigone* no longer qualifies as an ideal Aristotelian tragedy. It contains no tragic hero who because of some great fallibility is brought from good fortune to bad. Creon does not qualify because he is an out-and-out villain. Antigone does not qualify because she lacks the great fallibility.

It seems natural at this point to broaden our notion of dramatic tragedy. *Antigone* we might call a *sacrificial* or *heroic* tragedy, a dramatic work in which the self-sacrifice of a good person remedies evil, or promotes good. Aristotle is only half-right when he asserts that a pre-eminently good man should not be shown passing from good fortune to bad.

> Such situations are not just pitiable and fearful; they are incapable of fitting resolution.

The fall from good into bad fortune of the preeminently virtuous and just person through absolutely no fault of her own is incapable of generating a *catharsis*, a fitting resolution.[44] If justice really were to prevail, this kind of thing would not happen in the first place. But, *pace* Aristotle, we all know that in this world justice often does not prevail. Evil is often too powerful to be stopped without loss. Sometimes it can be blocked, or mitigated, only by sacrifice on the part of the good. Creon, when he gains power, aims a villainous attack at the sole survivors of Oedipus' bloodline. Antigone's plan is to respond to this attack in a way that has the best chance of defeating it and bringing

---

44. For more concerning the identification of *catharsis* in the *Poetics* with the kind of resolution a play has, see Daniels, *et al*, [1992].

him down. This end she is able to accomplish only by putting her own life on the line through unrelenting public confrontation. Her strategy does in the end cost her her life and fails to suffice of itself to achieve her goal. But it does succeed in laying the groundwork for Creon's downfall, which comes very shortly after her death.

If we limit the focus of our attention to just *Antigone*, we find an ideal Aristotelian tragedy with two tragic heroes. There are in *Antigone* only very slight hints of what we discover when we place the work in the wider context provided by its companion pieces, in which Creon transforms from hero to villain, Antigone into a better, more heroic, and far more complex person, and the play itself into a tragedy of a type which no longer conforms to the Aristotelian paradigm.

A Lesson in Honoring Tradition

and the Gods

In *Antigone* Creon overturns tradition and respect for the gods. By having the events of *Oedipus at Colonus* antedate those of *Antigone* Sophocles gives his audience a detailed lesson in how such matters ought to proceed. *Oedipus at Colonus* is replete with examples of care and attention given to worship, custom, and tradition. As the play opens Oedipus and Antigone unknowingly trespass into the sacred grove of the Furies.

> Stranger Now, before you ask for further information, come away from this seat! For you are on ground which it is not holy to tread upon.
>
> Oed. What is this ground? To which of the gods is it thought to belong?
>
> Stran. It is not to be touched nor to be lived upon . . .
> (OC 36-39)

Other locals appear and object to their presence within the sacred grove.

> But you shall not communicate these curses to me! You go too far (into the grove), you go too far! But so that you do not rush on in this voiceless grassy glade, where the bowl filled with water is mixed together with the flow of honeyed offerings, from there, O ill-fated stranger —

take every care! — stand aside, withdraw! Let a wide path separate you
from the grove! Do you hear, wanderer of many trails?
(OC 153-65)

Oedipus and Antigone agree to vacate the grove in deference to local
tradition.

Cho. A stranger in a strange land, O unhappy man, have the courage to
      hate what the city has come to hold as hateful and to revere what
      she loves.
Oed. Lead me then, child, to a place where, entering ground of piety,
      we may speak and listen, and let us not make war with necessity!
      (OC 184-91)

The local people find out who Oedipus is and begin to have second
thoughts about giving him shelter. Oedipus chides them,

. . . I beg you, strangers, by the gods, as you raised me from my seat, so
protect me, and do not, while you honour the gods, then send them into
darkness!
(OC 275-78)

Protection is finally advanced to Oedipus and Antigone, and Oedipus
must then set things right for having trespassed upon sacred ground,

Cho. Now make a lustration that is due to these goddesses, to whom you
      came first and on whose ground you trampled.
      (OC 466-67)

A description of the proper ritual follows in great detail:

Cho. First, from a stream that flows forever bring holy libations,
      touching them with cleansed hands!
Oed. And when I have this pure water?
Cho. There are bowls there, the work of a skilled craftsman; crown their
      brims and the handles on each side of the brims!
Oed. With olive branches, or woollen cloths, or in what manner?
Cho. Yes, take the newly-shorn fleece of a young lamb!
Oed. Good; and then, to what conclusion must I bring the rite?
Cho. Facing toward the dawn, pour your libations!
Oed. Am I to pour them with the bowls you speak of?

Cho. Yes, in three streams; and take the last one —

Oed. With what do I fill this? Tell me this also beforehand!

Cho. With water and honey; but do not bring wine to it!

Oed. And when the ground, darkened by overhanging foliage, has received them?

Cho. Lay on it thrice nine shoots of olive with both hands, and meanwhile make this prayer!

Oed. I wish to hear this prayer; for it is most important.

Cho. That, as we call them "Eumenides" (i.e., the kindly-hearted), as saviours they may receive the suppliant with kindly hearts: ask this, you and anybody who prays for you, speaking inaudibly and not raising a loud cry! Then come away without turning around! Do this, and I should take heart and stand by you; but if not, stranger, I should fear for you.

(OC 469-92)

One cannot imagine Creon taking interest in details like these in any way but hypocritically. At the end of the play, we have the following passage:

. . . he sat down by the hollow pear-tree and the stone tomb. Then he undid his sordid garments. And then he called his daughters and ordered them to bring water from a running stream for washing and libations to the dead. They went to the hill in full view, the hill of Demeter who tends young plants, and in a short time they brought their father what he had ordered, and they assisted him to bathe and to dress as custom prescribes. When he had got all the pleasure belonging to a doer, and none of the things he ordered had been neglected . . .

(OC 1596-1605)

Besides these intricate, detailed descriptions of ritual, the power of tradition and reverence figures elsewhere in the play. Oedipus hates the thought of meeting Polyneices, but Polyneices has petitioned at the altar of Poseidon to be allowed to talk with him, and Theseus says,

But consider whether his supplication compels you; consider whether respect for the god must not be observed by you!

(OC 1179-80)

Polyneices himself introduces this point of religious propriety when he appeals to Oedipus not to ignore him,

Daughters of this man, my sisters, you at any rate try to move our father to speech — he is a hard man to deal with, not to be addressed — so that he does not send me away — I am a suppliant of the god — dishonoured in this way, with no word in response!

(OC 1275-79)

The play lauds civilized behavior. Oedipus comments,

For among you alone of mankind I have found reverence and fairness and keeping to one's word.

(OC 1125-27)

At another point it is Theseus who gives the audience a lesson in civilized behavior,

Who then would reject the friendship of such a man, for whom, first, the common hearth of an ally exists among us forever? Then he has come as a suppliant of our gods and pays no small recompense to this land and to me. Out of respect for his claims, I shall never reject this man's kindness, and I will establish him as a citizen in the land.

(OC 631-37)

Theseus' words show generosity and wisdom. Twice during the play we learn that he has himself been observing the rites of worship at the nearby altar of Poseidon.

Not only does *Oedipus at Colonus* offer its audience a paradigm of respect for custom, tradition, and reverence toward the gods, against which Creon's management of events in *Antigone* falls woefully shy, in *Oedipus at Colonus* Theseus actually hauls Creon up short like a miscreant schoolboy and lectures him sharply,

For you have done things that bring disgrace on me, on your ancestors, and on your country. You have come to a city that practises justice and determines nothing without law; yet you have set aside the authorities of this land and have invaded in this way, and you take captive what you wish and subjugate by force . . .

(OC 911-16)

Yet Thebes at least did not teach you to be base; for she is not accustomed to rearing men to be unjust, nor would she praise you, if she learned that you are carrying off what is mine and what belongs to the gods, when by force you lead off their unhappy suppliants. Now, if I were treading upon your land, not even if I had the most just claims, without the permission of the ruler of the land, whoever he might be, would I either plunder or take captive, but I would know how a stranger ought to live among citizens. But you are shaming a city that does not deserve it, your own city at that . . .

(OC 919-30)

The events in *Oedipus at Colonus* not only satisfy our desire to know Oedipus' fate after the end of *Oedipus Rex*, they completely transform *Antigone*. Against it Creon cannot possible be viewed as a tragic hero, and Antigone's self-destructive, self-righteous behavior is seen to be much more reasonably motivated. We have already engaged in the legitimate exercise of isolating two of the three Theban plays, pretending that the others no longer existed and seeing what each contained in itself. It remains for us now to view the third, *Oedipus at Colonus*, in isolation.

IV

Oedipus at Colonus: Part 2

Let us sever all ties that connect *Oedipus at Colonus* with the two plays that bracket it. We now have no reason to doubt Oedipus when he claims repeatedly that he bears no guilt in the matter of his father's death and his marriage to his mother. In *Oedipus at Colonus* Oedipus' history is repeated for us in a brief, sanitized form. We must see him as a victim pure and simple.

For his part, Creon knows how to bury someone who cannot properly be buried in Thebes. But Creon, we learn, is a man who cares nothing about traditional or religious proprieties. He will ignore them if they stand in his way. And he *will* have his way.

What kind of play then is *Oedipus at Colonus*? All the details noted in the last section remain. The play still offers us a lesson in honoring tradition and revering the gods. As we remarked earlier, *Oedipus at Colonus*, while a serious play, is definitely not a tragedy in any way that approaches an Aristotelian sense. What kind of play is it? It is a play about a choice made properly.

About his long-ago parricide and incestuous marriage, Oedipus says to Creon:

O shameless arrogance, on whom do you think this insult falls, on my old age or on yours? To reproach me, you have spouted about violent deaths, marriages and calamities which I have borne to my misery, through no

choice of my own; for the gods wanted it this way, perhaps because they
were angry with our family from long ago.

(OC 960-65)

In the matter of where he dies and upon whom he bestows the
prophesied benefit of his burial, however, Oedipus does *not* view
himself as a straw blown by the winds of destiny, an innocent victim
who is made to suffer for reasons known only to the gods. When
Oedipus first visited the oracle at Delphi, it foretold that he would die
in a holy place sacred to the Furies and bring blessings upon those who
gave him shelter and honored his grave. Because of the honorable
treatment and sanctuary he receives from Theseus and his Athenian
subjects, Oedipus chooses to do all within his power to ensure that they
reap the benefit the oracle said will flow to those who shelter and bury
him.

During the course of the play, the people of Colonus and their king,
the legendary Attic hero, Theseus, behave generously, honorably, and
properly. They give the exiled Oedipus sanctuary and shelter, despite
the terrible opprobrium that accompanies him. There is no question but
that they deserve the blessing that Oedipus has it in his power to
bestow. Oedipus' determination to repay his benefactors is twice im-
periled in the course of the play, first by Creon and then by Polyneices.
Both men want to gain the bounty Oedipus' favor offers, Creon for
himself and Thebes, Polyneices for himself and Argos. Both men,
when they appear and make their claims upon Oedipus, clearly show
themselves to be unworthy, indeed, villainous. At the same time, with
the rescue of Oedipus' daughters from Creon's soldiers, Theseus and
the Athenians demonstrate by deeds as well as words that they are
worthy recipients of Oedipus' benefaction.

Oedipus Rex is a paradigmatic Aristotelian tragedy, whether we focus
just on the play itself or go beyond it to include the two other Theban
plays that are its "future". *Antigone* also qualifies as an Aristotelian
tragedy when the narrow interpretation is taken. But in a context which
includes the two plays which provide its "past", *Antigone* is not an
Aristotelian tragedy; it is what we have termed a *sacrificial* or *heroic*
tragedy. Finally, whether viewed by itself or in the company of the
plays that form its "past" and "future", *Oedipus at Colonus* is a serious
play, but not a tragedy of either of these sorts at all. It is a play which

is exemplary of *correct behavior* in the widest sense, whether in matters of courtesy, or tradition, or morality, or reverence to the gods. Whether Oedipus is, on the narrow interpretation, completely innocent, or in the Theban context, engaging in an understandable bit of self-deception about his innocence, he does his best to act correctly in dying. He condemns the villains for their villainy and bestows his mysterious dying benefit upon those who by their own words and deeds deserve it, Theseus and the people of Colonus and Athens.

Appendix

The following is a translation by Sam Scully[45] of the first passage of §13 of Aristotle's *Poetics* which was discussed in Part I. It is purposefully flat and interpretation neutral.

13. Following upon what has been said above we should next state what ought to be aimed at and what avoided in the construction of a plot, and the means by which the function of tragedy may be achieved. Since then the structure of the finest tragedy should be not simple but complex and one that represents fearful and pitiful incidents — for that is peculiar to this form of representation — it is obvious, to begin with, that good men should not be shown passing from good fortune to bad. This is not fearful or pitiful but repulsive. Nor again wicked people passing from bad fortune to good. That is the most untragic of all, having none of the requisite qualities, since it does not satisfy our feelings nor is it pitiful or fearful. Nor again the passing of a thoroughly bad man from good fortune to bad fortune. Such a structure might satisfy our feelings but it arouses neither pity nor fear, the one being for the man who does not deserve his misfortune and the other for the man who is like ourselves — pity for one who does not deserve misfortune, fear for the man like ourselves — so that the event will be neither pitiful nor fearful.

---

45. Daniels, *et al*, [1992], p. 210-211.

Bibliography

Adams, S.M. [1931]. "The Burial of Polyneices", *Classical Review* **45**, pp. 110-11.

_____ [1955]. "The *Antigone* of Sophocles", *Phoenix* **9**, pp. 47-62.

_____ [1957]. *Sophocles the Playwright*. Toronto: University of Toronto Press.

Bloom, Harold, Ed. [1988]. *Sophocles' Oedipus Rex*. New York, New Haven, Philadelphia: Chelsea House Publishers.

Brown, Andrew, Ed. [1987]. *Sophocles' Antigone*. Warminster, England: Aris and Phillips.

Bradshaw, A.T. von S. [1962]. "The Watchman Scenes in the *Antigone*", *Classical Quarterly* **12**, pp. 200-11.

Buxton, R.G.A. [1984]. *Sophocles. Greece and Rome*. New Surveys in the Classics no. 16. Oxford: Clarendon Press.

Daniels, Charles B., and Scully, Sam [1992]. "Pity, Fear, and Catharsis in Aristotle's Poetics", *Nous* **26**, pp. 204-217.

Dawe, R.D., Ed. [1982]. *Sophocles Oedipus Rex*. Cambridge: Cambridge University Press.

Dodds, E.R. [1988]. "On Misunderstanding the Oedipus Rex". In Bloom [1988], pp. 35-47.

Easterling, P.E. [1985]. *Sophocles*. In Easterling and Knox [1985], pp. 295-316.

Easterling, P.E., and Knox, B.M.W., Edd. [1985]. *The Cambridge History of Classical Literature: Vol. I: Greek Literature.* Cambridge: Cambridge University Press.

Ehrenberg, Victor [1968]. "Sophoclean Rulers: Oedipus". In O'Brien [1968], pp. 74-80.

Fagles, Robert, trans. [1984]. *Sophocles. The Three Theban Plays.* Introductions and Notes by Bernard Knox.   Harmondsworth, England: Penguin Books.

Goldhill, Simon [1990]. "The Great Dionysia and Civic Ideology". In Winkler and Zeitlin [1990], pp. 97-129.

Gould, John [1985]. "Tragedy in Performance". In Easterling and Knox [1985], pp. 263-81.

Gould, Thomas [1988].   "The Innocence of Oedipus".   In Bloom [1988], pp. 49-63.

Held, George F. [1983]. "Antigone's Dual Motivation for the Double Burial", *Hermes* **111**, pp. 190-201.

Jebb, Richard C. [1891]. *Sophocles, Antigone.* Cambridge: Cambridge University Press.

_____ [1966].   *Sophocles, the Plays and Fragments, Part I, The Oedipus Tyrannus.* Amsterdam: Adolf M.   Hakkert.

Kirkwood, G.M. [1988]. "Two Questions of Dramatic Form in Oedipus Tyrannus". In O'Brien [1982], pp. 63-73.

Knox, Bernard M.W. [1957]. *Oedipus at Thebes*. New Haven: Yale University Press.

_____ [1964]. *The Heroic Temper: Studies in Sophoclean Tragedy*. Berkeley and Los Angeles: University of California Press.

Lefkowitz, Mary [1981]. *The Lives of the Greek Poets*. Baltimore: Johns Hopkins University Press.

McCall, Marsh [1972]. "Divine and human action in Sophocles: the two burials of the *Antigone*", *Yale Classical Studies* **22**, pp. 103-17.

O'Brien, Michael J., Ed. [1968]. *Twentieth Century Interpretations of Oedipus Rex*. Englewood Cliffs, N.J.: Prentice-Hall, Inc.

Parker, Robert [1983]. *Miasma: Pollution and Purification in Early Greek Religion*. Oxford: Clarendon Press.

Pickard-Cambridge, A.W. [1986]. *The Dramatic Festivals of Athens* (2nd ed. revised by J. Gould and D.M. Lewis). Oxford: Clarendon Press.

Rehm, Rush [1992]. *Greek Tragic Theatre*. London: Routledge.

Rosivach, Vincent J. [1983]. "On Creon, *Antigone* and not Burying the Dead", *Rheinisches Museum* **126**, pp. 193-211.

Rouse, W.H.D. [1911]. "The Two Burials in *Antigone*", *Classical Review* **25**, pp. 40-42.

Storr, F., Trans. [1981]. *Sophocles. Oedipus the King. Oedipus at Colonus. Antigone*. Cambridge, Mass.: Harvard University Press. Loeb Classical Library.

Taplin, Oliver [1978]. *Greek Tragedy in Action*. London: Methuen.

Vellacott, Philip. [1971]. *Sophocles and Oedipus: a Study of Oedipus Tyrannus with a New Translation*. London and Basingstoke: Macmillan.

Vickers, Brian [1973]. *Towards Greek Tragedy*. London: Longman.

Whitehorne, J.E.G. [1983]. "The Background to Polyneices' Disinterment and Reburial", *Greece and Rome* **30**, pp. 129-42.

Winkler, John J., and Zeitlin, Froma I., Edd. [1990]. *Nothing to do with Dionysis? Athenian Drama in its Social Context*. Princeton: Princeton University Press.

Index

Index of Translated Passages

Oedipus Rex

Oedipus at Colonus

Antigone

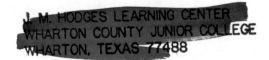